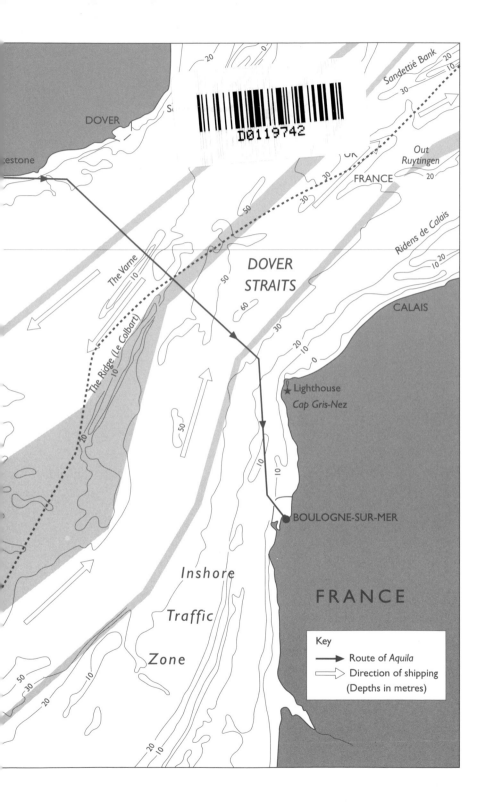

DOVER

estone

DOVER
STRAITS

Sandettié Bank

DOVER

UK
FRANCE

Out
Ruytingen

Ridens de Calais

CALAIS

The Varne

The Ridge (Le Colbart)

Lighthouse
Cap Gris-Nez

BOULOGNE-SUR-MER

Inshore

Traffic

Zone

FRANCE

Key

→ Route of *Aquila*
⇨ Direction of shipping
(Depths in metres)

Channel Crossing

By the Same Author

Allah's Mountains

Channel Crossing

One Man's Voyage around and across the English Channel

SEBASTIAN SMITH

HAMISH HAMILTON
LONDON

HAMISH HAMILTON LTD
Published by the Penguin Group
Penguin Books Ltd, 27 Wrights Lane, London w8 5tz, England
Penguin Putnam Inc., 375 Hudson Street, New York, New York 10014, USA
Penguin Books Australia Ltd, Ringwood, Victoria, Australia
Penguin Books Canada Ltd, 10 Alcorn Avenue, Toronto, Ontario, Canada m4v 3b2
Penguin Books India (P) Ltd, 11 Community Centre,
Panchsheel Park, New Delhi – 110 017, India
Penguin Books (NZ) Ltd, Cnr Rosedale and Airborne Roads,
Albany, Auckland, New Zealand
Penguin Books (South Africa) (Pty) Ltd, 5 Watkins Street,
Denver Ext 4, Johannesburg 2094, South Africa

Penguin Books Ltd, Registered Offices: Harmondsworth, Middlesex, England

First published 2001
1

Set in 12/14.75 pt Monotype Bembo
Typeset by Rowland Phototypesetting Ltd,
Bury St Edmunds, Suffolk
Printed in Great Britain by Clays Ltd, St Ives plc

A CIP catalogue record for this book is available from the British Library

ISBN 0–241–14077–3

pour A

Water is supple because it is incompressible. It slips under pressure. Pushed from one direction, it escapes in another. That is how water begins to roll. For water, the wave is liberty.

Victor Hugo

Acknowledgements

Many people helped me along the way on this voyage, both on land and on sea. Most are mentioned in the text, but special thanks are due.

For their professional skills and personal spirit, my agent, David Godwin, and publisher, Simon Prosser, have my admiration and gratitude. Thank you for seeing and believing. Thanks to Tony Smee of Solent Dinghies for sharing his knowledge, for his kindness and for ensuring that the business of outfitting my boat never felt like business. Thanks also to A. C. Smith and Lesley Levene for their sharp editing. For some of the documentation detailing the wreck of the freighter *Cita* I am indebted to *The Cita*, by Richard Larn and David McBride. Finally, I thank you, Adèle. Without you, I would never have arrived.

List of Illustrations

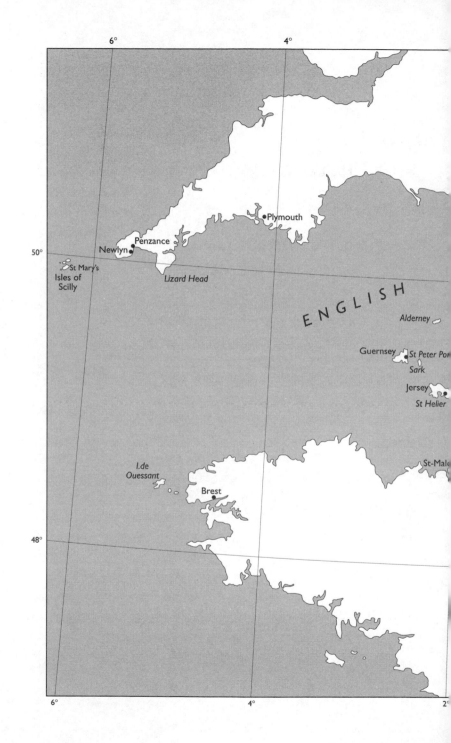

North Foreland

Folkestone Dover

Dunkirk

Dungeness Calais

Brighton Hastings Cap Gris-Nez

Southampton Eastbourne Boulogne

Bognor Regis Beachy Head

Portsmouth

Solent

Bournemouth

C H A N N E L

(L A   M A N C H E)

Dieppe

Cherbourg

Le Havre

Arromanches

Granville

Mont-St-
Michel

N

W E

S

| 0 | 10 | 20 | 30 | 40 | 50 | 60 | 70 | 80 | 90 | 100 |

Nautical miles

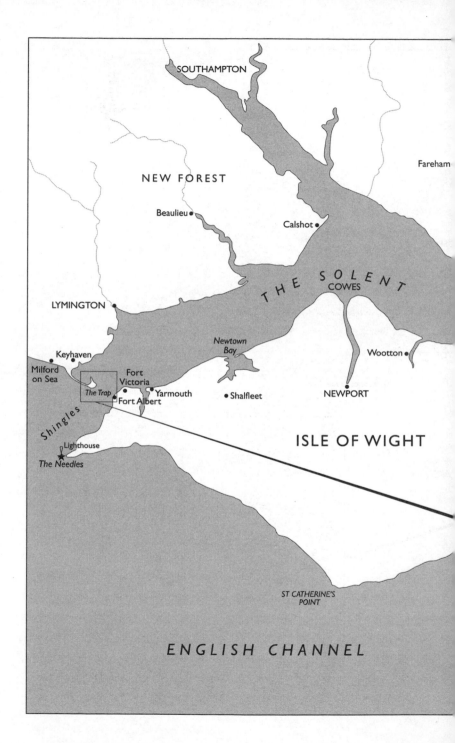

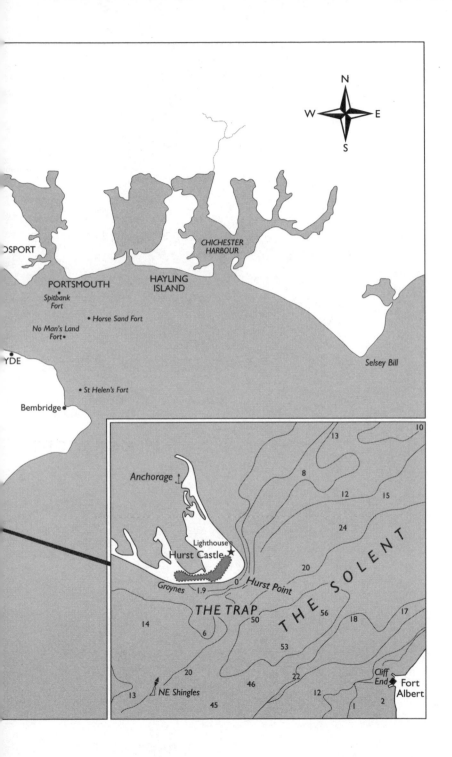

I

As a child, I dreamed of exploring the sea. Although we lived far inland in Devon, I made fields around our home the ocean and isolated trees in the middle of these fields my ships. Armed with a curved Moorish dagger that I took from the house and dressed in a piratical white shirt, I spent whole days out on the trees, the best of which had huge branches for sails and earth banks covering the roots for a deck. On these strange vessels, absolutely real as far as I was concerned, I criss-crossed the seven seas, and when I was told that every corner of the Earth had already been discovered, I didn't care a bit.

When I grew older, I still longed to explore, but never did go to sea. Every year buried the idea a little deeper, and by the time I returned from Russia and travels in the Caucasus mountains to take up a desk job with my news agency in London, the notion, like my childhood adventures, was forgotten.

One day a newspaper article caught my attention: the last lighthouse keepers in Britain were about to be replaced by computers. Lighthouse keepers were one of those features of the seashore I'd always taken for granted. But at the close of the millennium there were apparently only two manned towers left: one at the Lizard peninsula in Cornwall, the other at North Foreland, Kent. Soon these two would also be automated and their guardians, with their shiny-buttoned uniforms, would vanish. The story touched a nerve. So did an accompanying photograph of the Lizard's principal keeper, Eddie Mathews, a stoical-looking man with distant, brooding eyes. Even if for no other reason than I was dying to get out of the office, I picked up the phone and reserved a seat on the train from London to Penzance.

The day of my visit, an Atlantic storm blew down the throat of the Channel and the Lizard peninsula took the full brunt. This Cornish landscape had long since surrendered to the wind. Even the granite, even the flat fields themselves, seemed beaten into submission. Rain turned the dirt pathway from Lizard village parcel-wrapping brown and by the time I arrived at the lighthouse I was soaked. In recent months, visitors of every stripe – newspaper journalists, TV crews, tourists – had pestered Mathews for his story and he was not welcoming. I couldn't even feed his ego with another spread in a Sunday magazine or a spot on the lunchtime news; I was simply curious. For a moment I feared he'd send me away. 'No, that's all right.' His red, craggy face softened. 'Come in from the rain.'

I'd never been in a lighthouse before. This one had an unusual shape. Instead of the expected candy-stripe cone, it was a long low building with white walls, a dark slate roof and green doors running between two stubby towers, one of which housed the lamp. The building could have been a granite ship steaming along the cliff tops, the seven chimneys spaced along the central roof for funnels, the lamp tower the captain's bridge. Inside, every wall, pipe and door frame had been immaculately painted and polished, a shrine to an era when things were made to last – maybe for too long. Then there was Mathews's pride: the foghorn, a gleaming, out-moded piece of technology that was massive and delicate at the same time, like a performing elephant. 'It's the last one of that type in Britain. Works on the same principle as a flute,' he said. No one had thought to take down the fading chart entitled 'Soviet Submarine Classes, Soviet Amphibious, Communist Merchant Marine Identification'.

The son of a Cornish fisherman and grandson of a coast-guard, Mathews had worked the last forty years for Trinity House, the organization behind Britain's navigation marks. Nine of those years had been in the Atlantic lighthouse on Wolf Rock, where he'd lived with 100-mile-an-hour winds and waves that reached the top of the tower, where beds were built in a curve against the wall and supplies had to be brought in by boat. 'It could be like on a submarine when those waves hit us,' Mathews said. 'The whole thing shook like hell.' Now he was the last of his tribe. Again those melancholy eyes. 'All you're looking at now are cold slabs of granite. Keepers are the heart of the thing,' Mathews said. 'We're a seafaring nation, for God's sake.'

We spiralled up, climbing a narrow iron and brass staircase into the lamp tower. Two 1,000-watt bulbs burned, but it was the vast rotating lens of the lamp that did the work, hurling a flash of light twenty-five miles out to sea every three seconds. The lamp, lens and all, weighed a ton and burned with the power of 800,000 candelas, yet I could turn the whole perfectly calibrated mechanism with my little finger.

Through the lozenge panes of the lamp casing, the English Channel surged and rolled in streaks of green and white. To my surprise, the horizon was not empty: the blunt lines of several cargo ships emerged from the rain. Mathews said that something like 500 ships a day sailed up and down the Channel, while below its waters lay the wrecks of hundreds more. Even during a gale, this remained one of the world's busiest shipping lanes. 'I would have thought that this is the one place where it would pay to keep lighthouse keepers,' I said.

Mathews shook his head. Time was when lighthouses were all that stood between a sailor and the Channel graveyards like the Manacles, Needles, Goodwins or Scillies. The ruins of the first lighthouse in Britain, built by the Romans, still rose over Dover, and the last two manned lighthouses were also on the Channel, like candles at each end. But ships' satellite-positioning equipment had made getting lost a thing of the past and not only keepers but the 'signposts of the sea' themselves were becoming obsolete – you could almost switch them off.

A ghostly box, nothing like a ship, slid over the horizon. 'The Spanish ferry,' Mathews snorted, going on to scorn the captains of modern ocean freighters. 'They come out of Southampton, turn right, go to bed and wake up in America.' But I no longer focused on Mathews, or on the tower, or on the prisms of reflecting glass in the lamp, or even on the pirouette of the light itself. It was that scene of robot ships bustling through the storm that had my attention.

I'd always thought of the English Channel as the cradle of mariners and great journeys. The voyages of Captain Cook, the Pilgrim Fathers, the *Titanic*, Drake's circumnavigation, the D-Day armada, the evacuation by 'little ships' of Dunkirk: all these exploits started from south-coast ports, but what link did that past have with the lifeless scene at the Lizard, or anywhere else on the Channel, today? With the opening of the train tunnel even the old unshakeable idea that the Dover Straits made Britain an island seemed defunct. Taking the ferry, not long ago a reminder that we still depended on the sea, was on the verge of becoming quaint. Was Mathews not

6

only the last of his tribe but the relic of a whole sea we'd left behind?

That night I lay in my B&B room, an eighteenth-century attic over a cobbled street in Penzance, lights off, eyes wide open. My mind whirred to the banging of some door in the wind, the scrape of leaves against walls and outbursts of seagulls over the roofs. An energy that meant I'd never sleep penetrated the room, riding in perhaps on draughts through the cracks in the sash of the antique bay window. I drifted. For the first time in years, memories of childhood games returned: how alone I'd felt in the middle of those grassy seas; how I'd climbed into the branches of my tree ships to look for land; the magical sensation of being between one place and another, always on the move. And mingling with this reverie, restless images of Eddie Mathews, his granite tower and those great ships riding down the Channel.

Back in London, I began planning the voyage I'd always wanted to make. Never mind that people usually took sea exploration to mean seeking the north-west passage, rounding the capes or threading the islands of the Java Sea. I'd stumbled on a mystery much closer to home: the English Channel. If all the old images of the Channel seemed unimaginable now, as if in fiction, or stories from another sea altogether, what had come in their place? That was what I would find out. The unknown sea I'd dreamed of in childhood, I'd found it right here on my doorstep. I was going to explore the English Channel.

From then, my work as an economics correspondent became impossible. I thought only of going south to the coast, and on my way to work the seagulls wheeling over my bicycle seemed to urge me on. In lunch hours I walked by the Thames, watching cormorants dive for eels and the currents wrap like boas around the mooring chains of restaurant ships. And when I should have been writing dreary reports on the economy, I pored over a map of Britain and trawled computer archives under the key word 'Channel'. The day I told my boss I was leaving, he didn't look surprised. Neither did Adèle, the lovely French girl who would later be my wife.

For sure, this was not a journey I could make on land. No matter how much of the coast I traced, I'd never enter the heart of the Channel. For that, I had to go to sea – and not only go to sea, but to cross: my own Channel crossing. As a mountain must be climbed, an island circumnavigated, a fence jumped, so the Channel lays down its own challenge.

But how? Not only did I have no boat, I couldn't sail. Ferries were obviously too easy, yachts too expensive and complicated, and I didn't want to be a passenger on anyone else's yacht. The thought occurred briefly that I might try to swim, but I knew I'd never cope and, in any case, this was not for me. Swimming was a question of endurance, a struggle to force man's body into the fish's world, while I needed to live with, rather than fight, the sea. If only I could sail . . .

I'd have liked to walk down to the docks, a sack over my shoulder, to catch the tide at once. I dreamed of losing sight of land, of meeting great ocean-going ships, weathering storms and calms, reading the waves and currents, and scanning the horizon for some familiar lighthouse on the far shore. Then I could say I'd rediscovered the Channel; not the Channel of Eurostar, but the wild northern sea that Eddie Mathews knew so well and that we had come to ignore. When Adèle excitedly urged me to become 'a real sailor', I was filled with joy and dismay. That was my dream, but what chance did I have?

Clearly, before even getting afloat, I needed simply to escape London and head down to the sea, for only there, faced by boats, mariners and the Channel itself, my initiation as a sailor could begin. I turned to the map I'd taken to carrying in my wallet and scanned the Dover Straits, the white cliffs of Beachy Head, the Channel Islands and Cherbourg peninsula, the serrated coast of Brittany . . . The names were familiar, but not the places, for I'd been to barely any of them. My eye sailed hundreds of miles, roving back and forth, up and down. Finally, I stopped at those specks off the Cornish toe: the Scilly Isles. However one saw the Channel – lobster claw, funnel, crocodile jaws or, as the French say, *la Manche*, the sleeve – the opening began in the west and in that opening, as if about to fall in, were the Scillies. For ships arriving out of the Atlantic the Scillies would be the first sight of land, and for those on their way out the last. Who knew how I would continue, but this was where the Channel began and so, then, would I.

~

The ferry for the largest island of the Scillies, St Mary's, departed from Penzance. Stepping off the Great Western train, I was happy to be out of London again and back among the granite cottages, the shouting gulls and the bitter tang of sea air. Since there were no ferries on Sundays, I killed time by walking in bright sunshine to Newlyn, the port just along the sweep of Mount's Bay from Penzance. Newlyn had a large fishing fleet and there were many vessels inside the breakwater, although little sign of prosperity in the town.

A sundial over the door of a cottage near the harbour bore the inscription:

Time flys, Death haftes – a Moment
may be wish'd
when Worlds want
Wealth to
buy.

The shadow of the dial passed through the word 'Death'.

On the docks, stevedores in yellow oilskins and thick gloves wrestled crates of ice and fish from the granite quay into a refrigerated warehouse close by. A fisherman climbed from his boat across the decks of three others tied up together in a pontoon, then up the long rusty ladder that led from the mud of low tide to the top of the quay. I was startled, for he had exactly the same thin, kind face of the homeless man who stood outside my office in London selling the *Big Issue* – a homeless man who, as it happened, had also once been a commercial fisherman. This *doppelgänger* was a crew member on board the *Wayfarer* and he was getting ready for a ten-day trip for shellfish in the Irish Sea. 'I'm off to phone the boss about it now,' he said before walking away. I saw him return a few minutes later. 'The boss said no, we're not going. Said the weather's no good.'

I thought I must have misheard. After all, the sun was out, a pleasant breeze played over the harbour and the surface of the sea looked benign. Silently, I wrote off the captain of the *Wayfarer*. Even the cry of seagulls, it seemed, had turned from the usual wailing to mocking laughter. Perhaps the crewman could read my thoughts. 'The captain's old-fashioned and he'll ignore the weather reports if he sniffs the air and thinks otherwise. They could say it's bad, but he'll still go out. He also knows when to stay in. He's never wrong.'

Did this trust in the captain's nose mean that fishermen believed in the supernatural?

'Yes and no. I wouldn't say we're really religious, but we are superstitious,' the fisherman said. 'I won't wear green to sea. And if you see a vicar on your way down to the boat, then you must go back and start your trip again. A friend followed that rule once and got home to find his wife in bed with another man. Neither will you let your wife come down to wave you off. A whole crew out of Brixham was lost a few years ago after their wives waved them off.'

As I walked slowly back towards Penzance, I thought about how 100 years before, maybe less, the *Wayfarer* would not have gone out to sea on a Sunday whatever the weather. The Methodists in Newlyn took to rioting in 1896 to stop fishing on the Sabbath by trawlers that had come down from Suffolk. Some 100,000 mackerel were thrown back into the sea and much violence meted out before the army and navy intervened. Even in the 1950s and 1960s there'd been a few fishermen who refused to work on God's day of rest. They were gone now, and when I stopped in at the Fishermen's Mission chapel, I found the congregation that day numbered no more than a dozen. The pulpit was made from the full-sized bow of a wooden boat, with the lectern as a figurehead and written in gold around the bows 'Nevertheless, at thy word I will let down the net.' It seemed like something straight from the pages of *Moby-Dick*: the church where Ishmael, on the eve of his own voyage, sees a pulpit 'in the likeness of a ship's bluff bows, and the Holy Bible rested on a projecting piece of scroll work'. Even the sermon that evening, delivered by a retired merchant marine officer, was a variation on the theme of Jonah and the whale – just like that heard by Ishmael. The old seamen sang to piano and tambourine:

> 'Will your anchor hold
> in the storm of life?
> Will your anchor hold
> in the straits of fear,
> when the breakers roar
> and the reef is near,
> while the surges rage,
> and the wild winds blow,
> shall the angry waves
> then your bark o'erflow?
> Will your anchor hold
> in the floods of death,
> when the waters cold
> chill your latest breath?'

The voices were strong, the tune sad.

By the time I got back to Penzance, the tide was coming in. Waves licked the granite sea wall. Boats seemed to lose gravity as water lifted their keels off the mud. Families picnicking in the afternoon April sun retreated up the pebble beach.

That evening a storm hit. In Mount's Bay waves broke over the promenade where earlier ice creams and balloons had been sold, and the pavements ran with water. Thousands of pieces of seaweed hurled up by the waves littered the sea front and roofs of cars like debris after a bombing. It was then that I remembered having passed a vicar earlier in the day, a towering man with stern, pale eyes who walked quickly in the other direction.

Because of the storm, the *Scillonian III* ferry was cancelled two days in a row. I'd been determined to take my first step into the Channel by ship but could not remain marooned in Penzance indefinitely, so, grudgingly, I accepted the offer of an alternative. The light plane I boarded left from a field and shot out over the cliffs of Land's End.

From high in the air, the Scillies appeared as floating rocks. At a lower level, they looked like pieces of Dartmoor: scrubby grassland, granite piles, gorse and wind-bent trees. Only at ground level did the islands' famous softness and suitability for early flowers and vegetables become apparent. And although the islands are less than thirty miles from the mainland, with one foot in the Atlantic and one in the Channel, they felt much further away. When the prop plane broke through the cloud and patches of granite appeared in the sea, I wanted to change my watch.

A gale blew on St Mary's and the windsock at the airport stuck out like Pinocchio's nose. The sea moved in white mountains and from the runway we could see huge waves break against Samson, an uninhabited island some three miles to the west. Spray lifted into the sky with silent violence. *Thalassa!* Exhilarated by reaching the islands, those dots in the mouth of the Channel, I felt sure that I'd come to the right place. This was where – somehow – I'd find a way of becoming a sailor. This was where the path of my whole adventure began. In my joy, I wanted nothing more at that moment than to get on a boat and head seaward, up to Samson and the waves. I didn't care how rough it was. I felt invincible. Any kind of boat would do.

But when I asked at the harbour in Hugh Town whether anyone was going Samson way, I was answered with laughter. So, remembering a story I'd come across in Newlyn, I asked about the wreck of the *Cita*. The laughter stopped, then just as suddenly started again, but it was of a different sort. A boatman grinned: 'That was fucking something.'

Cita was a German-owned freighter that went down off St Mary's in 1997. When I'd first come across the story, I'd been surprised, thinking, in these days of safety measures and computerization, that major shipwrecks in the Channel had all but ceased to happen. The idea of ships like the *Cita* foundering around Britain seemed so primitive, old-fashioned. What had really caught my attention, however, were the remarkable events that had taken place *after* the vessel struck the rocks. Talking to many people on the Scillies, starting with the boatmen in the harbour, this was the story that I pieced together.

The *Cita*'s captain and his crew of seven, all Polish, set out on Tuesday of Holy Week from Southampton with 145 containers of varied cargo bound for Belfast. Seas and wind were moderate at first, but by the time the ship was in the western Channel the weather deteriorated to mist and drizzle with Force 6 winds. At about midnight, Captain Wojtkow passed the helm to the mate. It was then that the trouble began.

As with any well-equipped ship, *Cita*'s course had been programmed into a computer and the vessel put on automatic pilot. The mate began his watch by checking in the latest course, then settled back. Under standard procedure, he should have been accompanied by one other crew member, but the captain had allowed everyone to sleep. And so, with nothing to look at but the darkness of the sea and rain, and probably tired from having sailed and loaded cargo all week, the mate started to doze. The *Cita*, 3,000 tons in weight and just over 300 feet in length, sailed up the Channel like a ghost ship, her entire crew asleep.

At Land's End the course should have been changed to north, but *Cita* continued to sail westward through the mist for almost another two hours. Because a radar alarm meant to warn of any unexpected hazards had not been switched on, the vessel, which crossed two shipping lanes, could easily have collided with another boat. Or, had the course been just a few degrees different, the crew might have woken on Wednesday somewhere in the Atlantic. Instead, *Cita* sailed at full speed into the jagged eastern shore of St Mary's island, at a place called Porth Hellick. Without the alarm, which would have sounded at the approach of the Scillies, there was nothing to disturb the crew until 3.30 a.m., when they woke to the most terrifying sound a sailor can ever hear: rock tearing into metal. Water poured through a large hole in the ship's hull and she listed heavily to starboard, before settling on the seabed with about half her hull protruding from the water.

Almost immediately St Mary's volunteer lifeboat, the *Robert Edgar*, was on the scene and the crew were lifted off – one of them by helicopter because he had a broken leg. Captain Wojtkow, ultimately the man to blame, showed some style, staying on board until the wreck listed a dangerous seventy degrees, at which point he was evacuated, still wearing slippers. Before being flown to Cornwall later that day, he went to high ground overlooking the *Cita*'s grave and in tears gave a final salute.

Meanwhile, at Porth Hellick, a crescent of sand, black rocks and thousands of tiny orange, red and silver periwinkle shells, a crowd had begun to gather. Some were curious to see the ship before she broke up, but the eyes of most were not out to sea but on the shore, where with every hour the loose cargo of *Cita* was piling up by the ton. From the first few people in early morning, the numbers rapidly increased and before long much of the Scillies' population was on hand. Tourists joined in and, as news spread, so did hundreds more people from Cornwall, with reinforcements coming over on the *Scillonian III*. After a break of almost a century, the Scillies had just rediscovered an ancient and deeply satisfying practice: 'wrecking', or the plundering of stricken ships. Given the extraordinary mixture of cargo on *Cita*, what a bout of very good, if very modern, wrecking it was.

Crates of tennis shoes, checked Ben Sherman shirts, golf bags, anoraks and wooden doors – there was something for everybody. Children walked off festooned with strings of shoes, men clasped new tyres in each arm and women searched for their size in dresses. One container was filled with granite tombstones, quarried in South America, cut in India and due for undertakers in Belfast. The container sank at once, but some of the headstones were recovered later by divers and carved into souvenir clocks. Another container revealed computer mice, another raw tobacco, another twenty tons of tinned water chestnuts, another 1,500 wooden loo seats. In another were boxes of Irish leprechaun keyrings claiming to be made of brass. They were inscribed variously with 'The luck of the Irish', 'Lucky Irish shamrock', and 'As you slide down the banister of life, may the splinters never point in the wrong direction.' The fact of the shipwreck, the corrosive effect of sea water on metal and the itinerary of the *Cita* proved that the keyrings were neither lucky, real brass nor Irish.

Not all the containers held welcome surprises. One disgorged a million green and white plastic shopping bags destined for the Quinnsworth supermarket chain in Ireland. A message on the bags carpeting the foreshore called on shoppers to 'help protect the environment'. But there was a great deal to tempt the passer-by. Doors were popular. On the island of St Agnes, just across the water from St Mary's, the keeper of a minuscule shop showed me his new mahogany front door, but said he'd missed the best. 'I was busy doing my accounts and had my head down. Then I heard the farmers' tractors going by and I knew something must be up. But by the time I got down to the sea, they'd taken the lot. I managed to get a couple of doors that had floated in, but they'd been all over the rest.' Other wreckers were less ambitious. Margaret, the handsome and kindly wife of a local historian, did think about getting a door, 'because ours was from 1926 and could have done with replacing. But they were just the wrong size for our house – six inches too short.' So her husband, Alfred, every bit the bespectacled ex-schoolteacher and savant, made do with a new pair of swimming trunks. 'Oh, and the anoraks were great. The day or two after the wreck, when you went down the pub, everyone was wearing the same grey and black anorak.'

I wondered how I would have reacted. The morality of wrecking is ambiguous. In the mean days before tourism and flower growing, wrecks on the Scillies brought free wood and iron and, depending on their cargo, such things as weapons, cloth, food, wine and even treasure – anything that can be imagined to lighten a dark world in which the sea took more than it gave. 'When the news of a wreck flies round the coast,' wrote a certain Reverend Smith after travels in Cornwall in the nineteenth century, 'thousands of people are instantly collected near the fatal spot; pick-axes, hatchets, crowbars and ropes are their usual implements for breaking up and carrying off whatever they can. The moment the vessel touches the shore she is considered fair plunder, and men, women and children are working on her to break her up by night and day.' In the Scilly Isles, people once prayed 'not that wrecks should happen, but that if any wreck should happen, Thou wilt guide them into the Scilly Isles'. (In Tristan da Cunha in the south Atlantic, girls prayed for wrecks to bring young men 'so I may marry'.) Their prayers were often answered: the fifty-five or so visible islands and the legion of submerged rocks caused more than 1,000 (recorded) shipwrecks between 1305 and the end of the twentieth century.

At times, the law itself has been confused, inadvertently enticing the murder of survivors by stating that a ship could be stripped only in cases where all aboard had perished. 'If anything escaped alive, 'tis not adjudged to be a Wreck.' That statute dated from the seventeenth century, but it was quoted in self-defence as late as the mid-nineteenth century when two Scillonian wreckers threw overboard a dog, the last living creature, in order to lay claim to the ship. Under the modern Merchant Shipping Act, anything found on the seashore should be reported to the Receiver of Wrecks and then, after negotiations with the original owner, salvage money may be paid. If no owner steps forward before a year and a day, then the rights go to the finder. Not everyone on the Scillies was acting out of lust for free goods; Margaret was one of the many who collected, washed and bagged thousands of items of clothing to donate to charity. However, enforcing the rules was not easy. There are just two policemen in the Scillies, a constable and a sergeant, and only eight more were sent over from Cornwall.

The constant improvement of lighthouses, navigation, communication and charts has made the western Channel entrance relatively safe. There are now six lighthouses and one lightship (all unmanned) between the Scillies and Land's End, a distance of only twenty-eight miles. But until the 1750s, entering the Channel was vastly more fraught. Most charts wrongly showed the Scillies ten miles north of their true position. Also, the Rennel current, flowing northward from the Bay of Biscay, while not strong, was enough to queer the unwary helmsman's course.

One victim of this confusion was the British rear-admiral Sir Cloudesley Shovel, who in 1707 sent five of his ships and 1,648 men to destruction on the Scillies because he thought he was further south, closer to the French coast (a blunder which led obliquely to an enormous improvement in navigation, since Parliament then established a competition to find methods of measuring longitude at sea). The fleet's treasure sank in deep waters, where it lay until the 1960s, but Sir Cloudesley's body washed up almost immediately at Porth Hellick, the site of the *Cita* wreck three centuries later. After brief interment on the beach, he was taken to Westminster Abbey, but not before considerable damage to his reputation. Detractors said that, rather than go down with his flagship *Association* and his men, Sir Cloudesley had tried to escape with his friends, valuables and pet dog, only to be wrecked a second time off Porth Hellick and killed. There is an unproven story that a local woman years later confessed on her deathbed that she had found the rear-admiral half-dead on Porth Hellick beach and finished him off for his emerald ring.

The last good wreck, everyone on the Scillies agreed, had been as far back as 1910, when the New York–London liner *Minnehaha* ran aground on the island Bryher. Most of her cargo had to be jettisoned, including 243 head of cattle, Model-T Fords, grand pianos, sewing machines, carpets, shop tills, harmoniums, Panama hats and Old Judge cigarettes. Islanders are said to have smoked Old Judge for years after. Otherwise, twentieth-century wrecks, like the oil supertanker *Torrey Canyon*, on the whole brought nothing but trouble to the Scillies. *Cita* was a surprise that stirred many ghosts.

Almost half of *Cita*'s 145 containers were never accounted for, sinking off the Scillies or floating away to join the armada of containers already loose in the world's oceans. Some twenty tons of French wine were among the cargo that vanished. As for *Cita*, she lasted less than a fortnight before breaking in two and disappearing under the waves. I longed to see the wreck, even the outline, but it was too far out, so I walked instead along the beach of Porth Hellick. Despite the time that had passed, I didn't need to look hard for debris. Shredded bags, broken packing cases and fragments of plastic coat hangers emerged from the beach in all directions. Most valuables had probably been scavenged, but the deep, shifting sand no doubt held a few secrets yet. Poking from the sand and twists of blackened dry seaweed near my foot was a patch of checked red: part of one of those Ben Sherman shirts. To join the wreckers, symbolically anyway, I put the cloth in my pocket, smiling as I did so, until I remembered Rear-Admiral Sir Cloudesley Shovel and his ring. His monument, a boulder placed over what had once been his shallow grave, lay a short distance away.

★

Boats of every description inhabited the harbour of St Mary's – squat fishing smacks, spry little yachts, the trundling bulk of *Scillonian III*, buzzing Zodiac inflatables – but for me, a landlubber, they were all out of reach. To my great frustration, I remained a sea explorer with no way of even getting afloat.

Just to be on the water, I began taking trips from the port of Hugh Town on the big wooden motor launches that link the archipelago. Maybe seeing life on the smaller islands would give me ideas; maybe one of the islanders would be my guru, my old man of the sea, and tell me how I was meant to cross the Channel. However, on the launches I found myself sitting with tourist groups and on the islands I found people more interested in their tiny patches of land than the great, gaping sea. On Tresco, all paths led to the exotic gardens, while on St Agnes, farmers outnumbered fishermen and barely any of the few dozen residents even owned boats. No one was going to help me there. I could think only of going further out, hiring a private launch – just me, two boatmen and their dog – for St Helen's, an uninhabited island in the north. Here, if anywhere, I might find inspiration, I thought, for St Helen's had once been home to Celtic holy men, for whom long Channel voyages were something of a speciality.

Sitting that afternoon on the deserted island amid the ruins of an ancient chapel, I tried to imagine how this breed of sailor-hermits had managed some 1,000 years ago. Seeking the most remote islands and corners of the jagged coasts of Cornwall, Brittany, Ireland and Wales, they thought nothing of sailing up to 100 miles in some of the most unforgiving seas in the world. Moreover, often all they had to sail were coracles, basically dinghies made of wicker and animal hide and powered by oars. The larger version, a curragh, carried sails and could be made exceptionally seaworthy, as shown when a modern replica traversed the Atlantic in 1976, but it was still a boat of stick and skin. Legend related that some of these holy men and women had even more unlikely barques: a leaf for St Nolven, a millstone for St Warna, a rock for St Nimanauc and a boat of glass for St Petroc. But myths apart, the Celtic saints were extraordinary sailors, and the thought of their courage and faith as they criss-crossed the Western Approaches filled me with hope. Yet how, I wondered, was that really going to help me in my own Channel crossing? By the time I returned to St Mary's, still boatless, still a landlubber, I'd begun to think the whole thing might have to be called off.

For consolation I turned, as I had so often in my life, to swimming. I wasn't much of a swimmer, but I was a water addict. There'd been times when I couldn't pass a pond, river or stretch of sea without pausing for a dip. I'd swum in a Spanish tarn in the snow, a lake in Russia during thunder, a Mayan rock pool in the heat of Yucatan and a river in Chechnya as Russian rockets streamed over our heads into the hills. I'd abruptly stopped my car to get into ponds or rivers that appeared through the trees, I'd crossed the Hellespont, cleansed myself by the Delphic Oracle and swum at night in the Caribbean, trying to remember whether sharks slept or not. On hot days I liked to sit in an unplugged bath just to watch the silver flow from the cold tap. That was why now, as on every day I spent in the Scillies, I went down to bathe just by my B&B at a black and weedy cove known as Shark's Pit. To say I swam is a stretch, because the April sea was so cold, but by dashing out and back I could at least answer the call of water, a call that in the Scillies, which took their name from the ancient British water goddess Sulla, was too powerful to ignore; the islands themselves sink a few centimetres each year. Immersed for a minute or two, I came out red and renewed.

Near this place, Shark's Pit, there rose a copse of dinghy masts behind some sheds, and walking past the following morning, the sigh of wind in the rigging made me pause. For all my childhood dreaming, I'd barely been on real boats. As a young boy, I messed around in dinghies on a pond, but too little to learn any real skills. By my mid-teens, when I had the chance to spend a couple of summers on a yacht, I was too indolent to learn as much as a bowline, and, save the odd ferry, for the next fifteen years I didn't set foot on a boat again. That was the sum of my sailing experience.

The dinghies lay just metres from the edge of the water and they mesmerized me. Some were wooden and clinker-built, miniature Viking longships; others were plastic and little bigger than bathtubs. But in all of them the mast and rudder spoke of journeys – small journeys, yet journeys all the same. An idea grew. Could these little vessels possibly be the answer to my dream? Could I cross the Channel in a dinghy?

Now, I knew a dinghy was not meant for the open sea. Such a fragile vessel could easily capsize or fill with water. I might simply get lost. But unlike any other boat, I could afford a dinghy and surely, at least with a little practice, I could remember enough to sail one. After that, it would be just a matter of pointing at France and keeping going – the Celtic saints had managed in coracles, after all. Even if there was danger, I liked the scale: a small boat in a narrow sea made a big voyage, my voyage to rediscover a forgotten, bypassed world. The fragment of a prayer I'd heard long ago came into my head: 'Lord, the sea is so wide and my boat is so small . . .'

I held my breath, hardly daring to believe it; I'd cracked the problem. Now when I looked out at Hugh Town harbour and all the bobbing boats, it no longer seemed such a foreign place. The whole Channel was opening up and soon I'd be out there myself, part of the fraternity of Channel sailors.

In my euphoria, I craved to rent a dinghy right away for a celebration spin around the bay. In one of the sheds I found a man with a hunched back. Could I rent a boat for a quick sail? 'You have to be a member of the sailing club,' he answered. When I pleaded, he looked at me suspiciously. 'What sort do you usually sail?' I asked what he meant. 'Well, is it Toppers, Sunbeams, Mirrors or what?' I searched for the name of the dinghy I'd used as a boy, but realized I hadn't a clue. 'Well, quite a bit like those ones you've got out there,' I said. My inquisitor was pitiless. 'I'm afraid the boats here are for members only. Now, if you'd come in and said you knew how to sail a single-hander and you had a wet suit, I might have let you out as an exception. I have to be strict. The council has got something about people going off and getting drowned.'

The rebuff set me back. For a second, doubt intruded. What if I couldn't sail even a dinghy? What if a dinghy couldn't reach France? What if . . . There were many 'what if's, but I was soon on my feet. I'd found my path and my island pilgrimage was over. It was time to head east from the Scillies, east with the Atlantic flow and prevailing winds, deep into the English Channel, to search for my boat and the place where my crossing might begin.

I chose a fifteen-foot ten-inch open dinghy called a Wayfarer. There are more than 100 different types of dinghy and I didn't have much to go on, at first only a favourable magazine article about Wayfarers entitled 'Long-distance Dinghies' and the boat's look: neither overly technical, nor dumbed down; just classic, sturdy lines. A book called *Dinghy and Dayboat Directory* showed a picture of two Wayfarers sailing alarmingly fast, their two-man crews leaning right out over the water, their sails full to bursting. The text underneath, though, was reassuring: 'With built-in buoyancy, she is a very stable boat and difficult to capsize . . . a proven sea-kindly boat.' Somewhere else I read that two men once sailed a Wayfarer from Scotland to Iceland. Neither of them drowned.

Although I'd once imagined haggling by the shore, the small ad that seemed to fit my bill had been placed by a man near Oxford and so one morning I drove into the green hills, with cash in pocket and all the hope in the world. The Wayfarer stood on a trailer outside the garage where we'd agreed to meet. She had gleaming off-white sides, a deck of mirror-polished wood, a fat bow and a tapered stern. The name *Aquila* was stencilled on her bows. The word 'beautiful' entered my head and in the same split moment a wave of panic. How had I allowed my ridiculous plans to get this far? All that dreaming was fine, but this boat, this beautiful boat just in front of me, was real. To fool myself, I'd kept saying that a dinghy was nothing complicated, and maybe it wasn't, but all the same I was no sailor at all. The man at the shed on St Mary's, he'd known it, and I knew it too. As for those dinghies I'd sailed in childhood – they'd been cockleshells, half-coconuts, theatre props; the pond was a saucepan. I could no longer deny that. Now what did I plan? To sail across a sea, to sail out of sight of land, to go through waves and tides about which I understood nothing. A deep breath. It was not too late for a U-turn and the fast road back to London.

The next hour passed in a blur. The seller, who was called Rob, told me about *Aquila* and asked me what extra bits I wanted. To everything, I said 'Yes'. Very little of the pile of ropes, metal tubing and sails which came with the boat made sense. There was talk about 'bow fairleads', 'jib sheet cleats and tracks' and a 'tiller extension', all things I could barely picture. Even the basics baffled. The mast, for example, was riddled with pulleys and bits of wire, and to my horror when I peered inside the boat I could see no obvious place for it to go. The boom was meant to attach to something called a 'sliding gooseneck', but what that was I couldn't say. Rob displayed a tangled rope and wire device that I, had I been forced to guess, would have said was something for cutting cheese. 'The kicking strap,' he announced. The kicking strap? 'Yes.'

I handed over £2,000, hitched the trailer to my car and drove south.

As I approached Southampton, things looked up. I still felt like the shy schoolboy who isn't quite sure how he got the pretty girl to go with him to the dance – every time I checked my rear-view mirror, there she was, gorgeous and intimidating – but time cures all and the crisis had eased. Soon I'd arrive in Keyhaven, the out-of-the-way place on the Solent, opposite the western end of the Isle of Wight, where I'd found a boatyard to keep *Aquila*.

When I'd begun looking for a place to store the boat, the Royal Yachting Association provided me with an eight-page list of sailing clubs on the Hampshire coast. I'd thought I'd be able to take my pick, but getting a berth proved unexpectedly difficult – far harder than finding the boat – for I'd not counted on the cliquey nature of dinghy sailors.

'I'm afraid our waiting list is horrendous. It would be years before you got in,' the honorary secretary told me at the Keyhaven Yacht Club, the first place I tried. When I explained that I didn't want membership of the club, just to store my boat, he replied, 'You can't. You need to join.' The Eling Sailing Club told me I'd have to be resident within twenty-five miles of Southampton. The honorary secretary of Netley Cliff Sailing Club – one I picked in the mistaken hope that with a name like that oversubscription would not be a problem – told me that only Civil Servants could apply, 'though you could go on the waiting list'. At the Emsworth Sailing Club, the secretary asked in matriarchal tones whether I had anyone to propose and second me. 'What we do after that is invite you for a chat. It's not usually something that you do in a day or two. I'm afraid you've left it rather late.'

All these rejections induced an almost morbid fascination with the world of sailing clubs. The mother of them all, of course, was the Royal Yacht Squadron, whose building, the Castle, jutted out from the west side of Cowes harbour on the Isle of Wight. Here, having crossed one of the most exclusive thresholds in the country, I at least managed to have a cup of tea in the company of the secretary, Major Rising, RM.

Major Rising had a side parting ruthlessly enforced with some sort of cream, eyebrows that appeared to have been grown in an English country garden, a blue blazer with black buttons and shoes of dark suede. He was as imposing as the signpost on the jetty outside: 'Private landing place for members of the RYS and officers engaged on Her Majesty's Service'. Inside, the Castle smelled of wood polish, leather-bound books and Oriental rugs. Between gloomy canvases of past commodores and lords and admirals, huge swallow-like yachts plunged through oily green storms enclosed by heavy gilt frames. All that connected these princely vessels with the natty white fibreglass boats of today's members was the old privilege that went with the RYS: the right to fly – 'Wear, not fly,' Rising corrected me – the Navy's White Ensign. So how could one join? I asked. 'It's something you aspire to.' Rising's voice shook, pure basso profundo.

So I was astonished one day to hear the honorary secretary at the Lee-on-the-Solent Sailing Club say that I was welcome. 'We do have space and we will have more,' he told me over the phone. Yet the more about his fine club that the honorary secretary told me, the more determined I became to let the opportunity go. Hot showers and changing rooms, family discounts, functions, entertainment nights, a bar ... I just wanted a place in which to prepare my voyage. Too much bonhomie and regattas, I feared, and I would be distracted from my path; it was the Channel I wanted to get to know, not other dinghy sailors. Besides, what would they say if they found out about me, a novice, wanting to sail to France? They'd never understand, and I didn't want to have to explain.

That was when I discovered the Keyhaven boatyard. Several of the clubs I'd phoned had mentioned it as a sort of reject shop for people unable to join clubs, but as soon as I arrived I realized that this was in fact exactly what I'd wanted in the first place. The boatyard, tucked between a small road, marshland and a bay full of yachts and fishing vessels, was just a place to haul up boats, a plot of land that belonged to the sea. No commodores, not even a rear-commodore, my only obligation to pay a small monthly fee, and absolutely no need to tell anyone of my plans. About twenty yachts and fishing boats sat on the gravel and between them, like calves in a herd, lay another twenty or so dinghies, to which I added *Aquila*. Although a park for boats, nothing was regimented. Even out of the water, each vessel had her character and seemed to claim her own space. Some were undergoing repairs and several did not even have masts, while others looked all set to sail, as if just waiting for the Flood.

It was late afternoon when I arrived. The nearby car park emptied in sync with the ebb tide from the harbour, where boats nestled on the mud and curlews walked on stilts. A rainbow appeared over the Solent. There was much for me to do. The boat was still bound up in ropes and the boot of my car was full of gear. By a process of elimination, I had figured out how to raise the mast, but as in a children's puzzle was still trying to match each piece of gear to the place where it should go in the boat.

Footsteps on the gravel. I looked up and there was an aged man with the most intensely bright eyes. He had moon-white hair, damaged teeth and a paint-splattered set of blue overalls. He carried a power drill. I guessed the last car apart from mine in the car park, a battered white VW Polo, was his – it was his spitting image. But it was the blue eyes that drew my attention. They danced with life.

Later I found out that this was The Major, a Second World War tank commander who, though in his eighties, refused to give up sailing and was carrying out extensive work on not one but two wooden yachts. The boatyard seemed to be divided between people who thought he was mad to attempt so much at his age and those who admired his irrepressible energy.

'Good boat, the Wayfarer!' The Major didn't talk, he

shouted, but in a charming way that seemed to be the result of sheer excitement. 'Lovely job you've done on the woodwork!'

I began to say that I'd had nothing to do with the varnishing, but my words petered out. The Major had already marched back to his yacht, power drill whirring. I followed. The boat's name was *Nandhi*. She had one tall mast and a gently sloping bow and stern. Even my untutored eye could recognize a belle.

'What are you working on?' I asked.

'I'm planning to have a second mast put in. The sails are getting too big for me at my age, so I need a rig that's going to be more manageable.'

I asked about the name. 'Nandhi is a tribe in east Africa. The boat used to belong to one of our officials out there. He loved them and they loved him, so he named his boat after them.' The Major laughed his dry, high-pitched laugh. 'The thing is, I've heard that's also the name of a goddess and apparently she's going to be returning to Earth soon, so I don't know what that means for me!' More laughter.

I wanted to ask him about the Channel – was my plan feasible? The question had been on my lips since the Scillies, but I'd not dared ask, partly because I was afraid of the answer, partly because I guessed the dinghy fraternity would disapprove of such recklessness. But I felt at ease with this old man; he was a long way from the honorary secretaries.

'So you like the Wayfarer?'

'Yes. A good sea boat.'

I tried to look nonchalant. 'Do you think someone could get across the Channel in one?'

The Major paused for longer than I liked.

'Yes, I think you could. If you got the conditions right, I think you could.'

Major, I said to myself, thank you.

For my first sail in *Aquila* I'd only wanted an hour or so, but I wasn't given even that. The sea called my bluff and in an instant my dreams crumbled.

The day chosen was a poor one for beginners, wind sprinting and weaving like a rugby player, clouds drawn across a weak sun. But, of course, I didn't consider myself an ordinary beginner.

Things went wrong at once. When Adèle and I put *Aquila* in the water, the sails caught the wind and slammed the boat against the quay wall, her boom thrashing about as if possessed. The experience, which could easily have been avoided had we launched on the other side of the slipway, was unsettling, but finally we got away. The clattering row ceased, the mainsail filled and *Aquila* moved forward. But that peace ended abruptly; I couldn't steer the boat.

Several times I turned into the wind, the way I remembered from years back to change direction, but each time *Aquila* refused to turn, instead slowly swinging back into the direction we'd started from – away from the exit and across the harbour. Nothing responded and, out of control, we tore through the moored boats of the harbour. One near miss, another, then the inevitable collision, the victim a small blue yacht. I threw myself at the yacht to cushion the blow, but *Aquila* still suffered a scrape down one side; the yacht, thank God, looked OK.

The unfortunate Adèle and I stared at each other mutely. We were about fifty metres from where we had started and at a total loss what to do next. I clung to the side of the blue yacht to prevent us from going any further, but with the wind tearing at our sails even this was difficult. Two men on another boat moored nearby looked on with concern.

'Do you realize your rigging is all loose?' shouted one of them – unhelpfully, considering I didn't know what he meant. 'Why don't you take down your mainsail and just use the jib?' he continued.

I understood that. In fact, the same advice had been given in a sailing manual that I'd been reading back at the boatyard. The tiny triangular jib sail at the front of the boat would capture a lot less wind than the big main and so be easier to handle.

We hauled down the main and pulled up the jib. I let go of the blue yacht and we began to move off, but again, immediately out of control. I looked up and groaned. We'd attached the jib upside down. Seconds later, already at the far side of the harbour, *Aquila* ran aground. Miserable with defeat and sweating in my new oilskins, I took the oars out and began to row. The sea had no mercy. I had to pull against the tide and by the time we were back at the slipway my body also knew it had been beaten.

The following day, I called Jim.

Jim was another central character at the boatyard and, like The Major, would not lay down tools in his retirement. With his flat northern accent, trim body and fingers the size of raw carrots, Jim came across as a robust, serious man. But he had mischievous eyes, a stock of scatological jokes and, as he kept telling me, a 'lovely wife' to whom he'd been married for forty years. 'I know she's lovely, because she tells me so.' Jim said he was a tearaway in his youth, but, 'They knocked all that out of me when I did me national service.' I was sure he wouldn't harm a fly.

I had met Jim a few days after The Major and in the same way: when he came to admire *Aquila*'s varnishing. He must have assumed that with such a boat I was a sailor and proceeded to talk shop – tides, headlands, classic boats, races around the Isle of Wight. This was before my fiasco in the harbour and so, still bluffing, I'd nodded cheerily to every word. Only after could I admit to myself that I'd not understood a thing. This was a shame, as he was obviously a mine of information. Had he advised me to sail out into the Solent when the tide was coming in or the other way around? Whichever way, it apparently made a big difference. He even had a maxim by which to remember, but was it 'in when out' or 'out when in'? With a mental shrug of the shoulders, I decided the main thing was to make sure he never discovered quite how ignorant I was.

Now, my pride washed away in the harbour of Keyhaven, my plans in pieces, I only hesitated a second, purely from embarrassment, before picking up the phone.

'May I speak to Jim?'

'There's two Jims here. Jim the boatyard owner and Jim on the lathe. I'm Jim on the lathe.'

I knew the voice. 'Do you remember me? I'm Sebastian with the Wayfarer and the varnishing.'

'Oh yes, that's right.'

And I gave him the whole story – how I'd thought I could get away with it; how I'd hoped to pick things up as I went along; how I'd just wanted to nip out into the Solent and back, but ended up never even leaving the harbour. The only thing I didn't mention was wanting to cross the Channel.

Then I asked him straight: would he give me a lesson or two? All I needed was a start, just enough to get going, and I would pay.

'I won't do that for money, Sebastian. I like to go out for a sail every now and then. That would be no problem at all. I'll show you the basics and, as you say, get you going.'

I wanted to kiss the man.

Lesson one was that, in sailing, precision matters.

My attempts to rig the boat – in other words to put up the mast, the wires that hold up the mast and the sails – had ignored this rule and, as a result, we'd lost control. For example, there is a lever on the mast which I did not use, purely because I had no idea what it was for. Because the gadget, about the size of a tin opener, looked so insignificant, I thought I'd just ignore it. As it turned out, this was the device for putting great tension in the wire that holds the mast to the bow of the boat. Because this wire was left slack, so were the other two wires holding up the mast, one on the left, or port, side, and the other on the starboard, or right. The effect of so much loose rigging was that the sails, which not only power but also help steer the boat, were ineffective. 'Do you realize your rigging is all loose?' The words echoed.

The next lesson, though, was that attention to such details was only a start, for learning to sail is like learning a language: it means accumulating facts, but also adopting a system and, in the end, a culture. My rigging problems would soon be behind me, but there were any number of other practical skills to learn, and learn so well that they became automatic. And even then, all I'd know would be the boat, when understanding the sea and sky was just as important. Matters as basic as tides remained beyond me. When I asked Jim how the tide worked, he chuckled at my presumption. 'It's all to do with the sun and the moon,' he began, and I laughed too. This wasn't something I'd learn in a day. Nor how to understand the shape of waves, to survive in a storm, to navigate with no land in sight or even something as simple as tying two ropes together with a knot that wouldn't slip yet was easily undone. The idea of my crossing had come so easily, but at that moment the Channel could not have seemed wider.

At last, it was time for *Aquila*, the sea and I to be reintroduced.

Jim sat in the bow and gave instructions, I sat in the stern with the controls. I'd half expected a repeat of that first experience, but something new was apparent as soon as we left the quay. This same boat that had seemed of concrete when I'd rowed and hauled her out of the water in despair a few days earlier was alive – truly alive. All fifteen foot ten simply leapt through the harbour, and the water that had been like glue was now slick. We skated.

The controls for the mainsail jumped in my hand like the reins of a horse. Underneath, the sea rushed and laughed. When the boat tipped away from the wind, we compensated by leaning back, jerkily at first, then finding the balance. Out in the Solent, the sudden width of water dazzled me. Gusts of wind jumped from nowhere. Spray shot off the bows. For the first time, I knew what it was not just to sit in a boat but to become part of it.

'You know,' I shouted, 'I like this boat.'

Those first weeks of summer my world expanded with every day. I was still in London with Adèle, but I lived for the south coast, a commute of two and a half hours from the city.

Keyhaven lies at the mouth of a small river, Avon Water, which trickles across mud flats and meets the sea at the western limits of the Solent. At high tide, sea water floods the flats, making a broad area navigable by small boats, but at low tide just the river and glistening mud are left. Between the harbour and the Solent is a lonely bay, protected by a long shingle bank and disturbed only by the cries of seabirds.

At one end of the bay squats Hurst Castle, which started as a rose-shaped Tudor keep but had ended up a grim, low artillery platform. At the other end is a small opening into the Solent, where the water immediately becomes choppier and the winds stronger. After two lessons with Jim, Adèle and I were able to sail out of the harbour on our own, but we'd go no further than just out of the bay and back. The rest of the Solent stretched eastwards, seemingly for ever. To the south was the Isle of Wight; immediately to the west was the narrow opening to the sea. This opening, with Wight on one side and the front of Hurst Castle on the other, was known as Hurst Narrows, dominated by the Trap, a place of fierce currents and turbulence that we were strongly advised to keep away from. Beyond, invisible, was France. I was far from confident. Although these outings were a huge improvement on our first day, the mix of confusion, fear, excitement, hope and occasional despair never seemed to alter, while the simple fact that we could sail only in such reduced and protected circumstances underlined how much there was still to learn.

Jim taught me many things about sailing, but in essence that balance is the key, governing the speed, safety and manoeuvrability of the boat. As dinghies go, *Aquila* was not considered overly complicated, but to me she appeared to be a floating bucket of pulleys, poles, ropes and shackles. Jim tried to explain the method in the madness, pointing out the symmetry of all the gear. Straight down the centre were lined the crucial elements for power and steering – rudder, centreboard, mast and boom – while mirrored to left and right was the supporting rigging. The trick though, he said, was to turn all these components into a single instrument, then make that instrument work in harmony with the sea and wind. Boat, elements and man were a triangle that had to be able to balance on any of its three points and only when that balance was achieved did the boatman become a sailor. I could take in only a little of this at first and one major element always seemed to be out of control.

The immediate task, of course, was to keep the boat upright. This is more of a problem in a dinghy than on a yacht, since dinghies do not have a keel, a heavily ballasted fin that protrudes deep into the water from the bottom of the hull, giving the vessel a low centre of gravity. The keel, often filled with lead, is so heavy that even if the wind could push the boat on to her side, the keel would more than likely pull her back up again. The same principle is behind those children's toys that can be knocked over but won't stay down. The advantage of not having a keel is that dinghies can negotiate shallow water, and they can be taken out of the water and put on a road trailer in minutes, ready for transport anywhere. (One of the most famous sixth-century Celtic holy men, St Samson, was said to have a coracle small enough to put on a chariot, but large enough to then carry the chariot.) But not having a keel also means inherent instability in strong winds, forcing the sailor to sit near the edge of his dinghy and lean out as far as necessary to maintain the boat's balance. If the wind blows the boat over on to her port side, the sailor must sit on the starboard, and vice versa.

This much was easy to understand, although mastered only by trial and error. The second basic technique to prevent capsize took me into more complicated areas, where the mere mention of knots filled me with apprehension. After all, I was still at the stage where, for an hour of sailing, I took two hours to put *Aquila* together and afterwards another hour to take her apart. To tie a bowline, one of the most frequently needed knots on a boat, I still had to inch my way through the story of the rabbit coming out of its hole, going round the tree and disappearing back down the hole.

The balancing technique in question was reefing, which is to reduce the size of sail area by lowering the sail and reattaching the now smaller triangle to the boom. The reduced sail gives the wind a smaller target and makes the boat easier to handle, so on a lazy summer's day the sails would be full, but in a gale only a tiny handkerchief would be left, and theoretically in both cases the boat should be equally balanced. Jim demonstrated reefing with a few deft turns of rope that left the once giant mainsail half its size, the surplus canvas at the bottom neatly collected and wrapped up around the boom. 'That should help you manage things out in a strong breeze and then, when the wind drops, you just shake out the reefs and sweat your main back up,' he said. Thankfully, he left his work in place, since however easy he made it sound, I was sure that once the reefing was undone I'd never figure out how to reduce the sail again.

The big danger moment was in the tack, that is when changing the direction of the boat in order to zigzag forward against the wind. When this happens, the sails swing over to the other side of the boat, meaning that the sailor, still holding the tiller and ropes that control the sails, must move rapidly to the other gunwale before the dinghy can tip over. Not infrequently my coordination failed and instead of ducking on to the other side, I'd fall on my back, let go of the tiller and send the boat spinning like a bronco, one degree from capsize. In all these early forays I was assisted by Adèle and I often wondered how I could possibly manage alone. Even with two of us every manoeuvre was a test. Still, Jim was always ready with advice in the boatyard and so was a copy of the handbook *Sailing: A Beginner's Guide* that I'd bought in London and tried to read a little of every day. Gradually, we began to hold our own in *Aquila*.

Waiting for our third and what was to be final full lesson with Jim, we decided to drive up the coast to Barton-on-Sea for a swim. Herman Melville, who wrote in *Moby-Dick* of the 'water gazers' and dreamers who have no business on the water yet still gravitate to the shore, would have recognized the scene that we found there. 'These are all landsmen; of week days pent up in lath and plaster – tied to counters, nailed to benches, clinched to desks,' he wrote. 'Strange! Nothing will content them but the extremest limit of the land; loitering under the shady lee of yonder warehouses will not suffice. No. They must get just as nigh the water as they possibly can without falling in.' In the mid-nineteenth-century world, without cars, planes, space rockets, television or Internet, seafaring was incomparably exotic. But even today the waves draw us to the sandy rims of space, to stare into the unknown. Even at Barton-on-Sea: lads with black T-shirts and red arms; an old couple in fold-up chairs, he with dark brown cords and leather sandals, she with a white hat and tartan rug over her knees; local beauties hoping to change their milky skin, but not quite daring to go topless – all of them sitting and staring at the blank sea. Behind this front line, like heavy reinforcements, sat the inhabitants of the green, red, yellow, white and blue beach huts. They drank tea brewed on tiny stoves and also stared at the sea. With the sun above and cliffs behind, there was only one way to look. Still more reinforcements came: a man and woman exhausted already by the sun ('It's OK, we can take shelter in the car,' I heard him say); a group of people with Down's Syndrome, at once clumsy and intensely conscientious as they tried to throw their ice-cream wrappers into a bin; a troop of tiny women with permed white hair on a shiny bus called 'Whippets'. I too sat on the sand and stared, but wished I was out there: water's edge held no attraction for me now; even swimming had ceased to be enough.

That afternoon we set sail, reefed as far as possible despite the light winds, rather as if we'd driven on to the motorway in second gear, but a guarantee that we'd stay in control. Jim, sitting in the bow and wearing a floppy blue hat against the sun, seemed to be proud of his pupils, but whenever I tried to press him on how he gauged our progress, the canny old fellow was not quite as effusive as I'd hoped. When I suggested nipping across to the Isle of Wight, he answered drily, 'Not today, I don't think.' On the way back into Keyhaven, he said in a matter-of-fact way that I'd probably need two seasons to become a competent sailor. 'What you really need in any case, Sebastian, is to go on a proper course with the RYA or something.' I kept the veneer of grateful pupil, but inside I seethed. Two seasons and a course alongside school brats – this was not for me. I'd already set in my mind that I'd be crossing the Channel the following summer. My crossing was an idea that had come as if in a dream and to be shouted at through a teacher's megaphone or to have to wait more than a year would wake me.

I realized that nothing could be the same with Jim from now. Unless he knew about my plans – that I was learning not just to sail but to cross a sea – he'd never understand what kind of help I needed. I wanted badly to take him into my confidence, but I couldn't. Jim was a joker, but he was also a proud man who'd worked hard for the fun he'd had in boats, and I was afraid he'd not understand, or even be offended by what he might think was my cavalier approach. At the very least, he'd think I was crazy.

So I'd have to do without Jim and learn on my own. He'd given me the basics and now I'd take my *Beginner's Guide* and work through it page by page. It began with a chapter on wind direction and ended 200 pages later with navigation. After the initial fright, I was almost glad that my hand had been forced. I was on a voyage after all and Jim couldn't shepherd me. I was the captain of my boat. When we got back into the boatyard, The Major was, as usual, doing something to his yacht. 'Take that hat off, Jim, you're going to push up prices in the boatyard!' he shouted, laughing so that we couldn't help laughing with him. That was the last I saw of The Major. Shortly after, he put *Nandhi* back in the water and sailed her to another port; boat owners, like their boats, could not be tied to the ground for long. I saw Jim around the boatyard, but we never sailed together again. The plan to sail to France was a secret between *Aquila*, Adèle and me.

One of the first things I'd done after buying *Aquila* was to pin a nautical chart of the English Channel above my desk in London. I hardly understood a tenth of what appeared, but for me the chart was a thing of beauty. Ordinary maps show the sea blank and land full, but on nautical versions the situation is reversed. On Admiralty chart 2675, mustard-yellow southern England and northern France were empty except for coastal towns and a few mysterious symbols. But the sea, shown in blue, then light blue further out and white after that, contained all the symbols normally appearing on land – contour lines, place-names, shaded-off no-go areas, even directions for traffic – and a great many others that I could not decipher. This was my treasure map: it showed me where to go and, if I could learn to read its secrets, a way to get there.

Written in purple, the warnings EXPLOSIVES DUMPING GROUND off Brittany and SUBMARINE EXERCISE AREA off the Cornwall and Dorset coasts caught my eye at once. So did the fat, purple exclamation marks that a check in the seventy-page key to Admiralty charts told me meant light-house. Next to every beacon was also written in code a brief note. The Beachy Head lighthouse, for example, had 'Fl (2)20s25M, Horn (1)30s', meaning, I read in the key, that there would be two flashes of light every twenty seconds visible from twenty-five miles and in fog a horn blast every thirty seconds. Mostly, though, I began simply by examining the depth indications. These small-print numbers were the most easily understood symbols on the chart and the most common, swarming like numerical fish up into every corner of the Channel. The detail was staggering, drawing attention to the most minute of changes, such as 16.8 metres at one spot between Hastings and Dieppe and 19.2 metres off Selsey Bill. Almost as if playing dot-to-dot, I followed the depth contours, slowly drawing a mental picture of what happened under that pan-flat surface of the sea most of us knew.

The first thing that stood out was how shallow the Channel was, its maximum depths only a small fraction of those in the

Atlantic, or even the Mediterranean. The second point was that the contours of the Channel bed had a definite pattern, as if there ran between England and France an underwater valley downhill from the Dover Straits all the way to the Atlantic. The valley's depth below sea level fell steadily from an average of about twenty–thirty metres in the area from the Dover Straits to Beachy Head, to about fifty–sixty metres until after Salcombe, then sinking from seventy to about 100 metres at a line between Ouessant and Land's End. Most of the way, the drop from beaches was gentle, but at Cornwall and Brittany the valley walls tumbled almost instantly to about seventy metres below the sea.

In prehistory, this now hidden valley really did exist, dry land that linked Britain to the rest of the European continent. The mirror coastlines of France and England – granite in Brittany and south-west England, Jurassic in Portland and Calvados, and the soaring chalk lands of south-east England and Pas de Calais – tell the story. At the eastern end, the valley connected to the dry plain that would eventually become the North Sea and at the western limit it met the Atlantic somewhere well beyond Land's End. Running down the centre of the valley was a river into which drained the rivers of southern England and the Paris basin before emptying into the Atlantic.

The western part of this valley was flooded by the Atlantic deep in geological history. However, an isthmus more or less between Dover and Brighton on one side and Dunkirk and Dieppe on the other survived long into human existence. Where ferries now sail, men hunted woolly mammoths, giant elks and other fantastic beasts over downs that stretched uninterrupted from Kent and Sussex to northern France.

People would almost certainly have lived on the high ground, the same places that would later become the white cliffs, but they may also have lived inside the valley, next to the river, for example, or under the oak trees whose ancient acorns have since been found on the seabed. Between 8,000 and 10,000 years ago, just when the wild hunters first began to mellow into Neolithic farmers, the seas started to close in. When the last Ice Age came to an end, the ice sheets crushing northern Europe went into retreat, rearranging the landscape of the Channel region and leading to the flooding of the Anglo-German plain. The remains of the Anglo-French valley were reduced to an ever-decreasing land bridge in the Dover Straits, battered on one side by the North Sea and on the other by the Atlantic. As the chalk bridge came under pressure, generations of men in the area must have felt the ground grow wetter before finally the connection broke.

Once breached, even slightly, the gap must have broadened rapidly under the pressure of sea water tearing from north to south and back north, and in the last centuries of the sixth millennium BC the valley was irrevocably divided. Although still a different shape from today, Britain was an island. What archaeological evidence there is suggests that men took to the sea in the very earliest times. Well into modern history many parts of the world, England among them, were more dangerous or difficult to reach on foot than by boat. But although there'd long been men rowing simple boats such as coracles or canoes off southern England or northern France, someone must have been the first to cross after the land link had been finally breached. The first true Channel-crosser.

Traces of the valley and the time when Britain and France were joined are easily found both above and below water.

The shallowness of the Dover Straits is reminder enough. The Goodwin Sands, just north-east of Dover, emerge right out of the sea at low tide, dry enough at times to play cricket on. There, the chart showed that depths shrink abruptly from thirty metres to ten to zero and colouring switched from white to blue, then green, which signified tidal land. Numerous other underwater hills clutter the straits and each of them was named on the chart, just as features like rivers are given an identity on maps of the land. The Sandettié bank rose to ten metres below the surface, as did the Varne and Ridge banks. The Vergoyer, close to Boulogne, undulated between seven, ten and 4.2 metres below the surface. Then, near the Channel Islands of Alderney, Guernsey, Sark and Jersey – themselves the peaks of what used to be high ground at the edge of the valley – the chart showed a large area named Hurd Deep. Here, the surrounding depths of between fifty and eighty metres fell suddenly to between 120 and 174 metres – a hole that in the days of the river was once a lake. Other echoes of the drama are less obvious. A peninsula that had been an integral part of northern Europe's ecology was separated, so herds of larger beasts still living on the Continent became extinct in Britain, while more modest creatures became stranded on the islands. The Scillies have a shrew, the *Crocidura suaveolens*, found nowhere else in Britain except the Channel Islands, while Jersey claims a unique toad not found even on nearby Guernsey.

Shifting water levels and erosion continue to alter the landscape to this day. This is a work in progress that is reflected in many folk stories about flooding over the years, stories which, although unscientific, do give some indication about just how recently changes have come about. One account from Jersey relates that the island was so close to France that the visiting Bishop of Coutances used to bridge the gap with a plank, until in the eighth century a three-month storm 'gathered the waters from the Ocean in such quantities from our coasts that the March tides overstepped their ordinary limits and overwhelmed a large stretch of country'. According to John Twyne, a dignitary in Canterbury at the start of the sixteenth century, the Goodwin Sands were 'very fruitful' and with 'much pasture' right up to the Roman period, after which a terrible storm 'drowned' and 'overwhelmed with sand' this supposed island. Another story dates the Goodwins' inundation to 1099, when, we are told, the new hazard claimed as its first shipwreck victim Earl Godwin, hence the name. Sadly, this conflicts with the more accepted version of history that says the earl in fact died more than forty years earlier, choking during dinner with Edward the Confessor.

Ancient tales of an entire underwater civilization off Land's End persist, even when this is one of the most closely charted pieces of sea in the world and, to date, nothing out of the ordinary has been found. Lyonesse, according to tradition, was a Christian land of plenty that stretched between Cornwall and the Scillies, including 140 villages and churches and a great town on what is now Seven Stones reef. 'People assert that there was a land, Lionesse, so-called from some fable or other, covered over by an inrush of the sea,' William Camden wrote in 1586, and more than four centuries later the case has not greatly advanced. Stories of sailors hearing bells and seeing rooftops below the water, and the occasional discovery by a fisherman of bits of masonry or crockery in his nets, are about as far as the evidence goes.

The Poet Laureate Alfred, Lord Tennyson came away from

a five-day trip in 1860 supporting the idea that the Scillies were not only part of Lyonesse but also the site of the equally mysterious Avalon, where King Arthur was taken in a 'dusky barge, dark as a funeral scarf', after being mortally wounded in battle with Mordred. Since then, the Scillies have claimed the king's supposed tomb, a rock showing the indentations of his fists, and, as Steven Ottery, the curator of St Mary's museum scornfully recounted, 'one where Arthur's dog put his paw'. Lyonesse, if nothing else, is a city of dreamers. In a strange and little-known parody by H. G. Wells, *The Autocracy of Mr Parham. His Remarkable Adventures in This Changing World*, Lyonesse becomes the setting for a secret poison-gas factory and lunatic plans to take over the world, while in the late 1990s a Russian professor claimed that the lost city in question was not Lyonesse but Atlantis. Eschewing the usual searches for Atlantis in the Sea of Marmara, the Canaries and even the Bahamas, Professor Vyacheslav Koudriavtsev, from the Institute of Metahistory in Moscow, homed in on Little Sole bank, an underwater hill and fishing ground just beyond the Scillies. His case was never proved and some islanders, mindful of the giant Soviet factory ships that used to steam down from Murmansk and clean out the mackerel stocks, muttered that the story was just a cover for something less wholesome. The usually sceptical Mr Ottery reckoned a Russian nuclear submarine lay wrecked on the seabed. Surely more people would know? 'Oh, it's all hush-hush,' he said.

Such legends, though, may not be totally groundless. An underwater ridge shown on the chart proves that there was almost certainly once land between Cornwall and the Scillies, although the flooding of this ridge is said to have taken place long before any kind of Lyonesse could have come into being. A more promising possibility is that the legends refer to communities wiped out when the Scillies, originally one big island, were flooded and turned into an archipelago. This happened comparatively recently and so it is entirely possible that settlements of some sort were destroyed. Ruined walls have been found under the water between the islands, but whether these are magical dwellings, remains of a Bronze Age village or something as mundane as abandoned oyster farms depends on whom one asks.

Yet of all the secrets of the old Channel valley, the greatest and most real was literally prised from the sea by a French scientist called Aimé Thomé de Gamond, who discovered the existence of an unbroken bed of chalk across the Dover Straits. Chalk is easily cut but remains stable, and although soft is impervious – in other words, it is the perfect material for tunnelling. Circumstantial evidence, notably the white cliffs on both sides, pointed to the chalk link, but in the 1850s Thomé de Gamond became the first to be sure, and his discovery, made during perilous skin dives, opened the way for the building of the Channel Tunnel a century and a half later. The chalk was so convenient that it seemed almost to be there by design, as if the gods of the Channel had always planned a tunnel in reserve, a hedge against their experiment of making Britain an island.

Numerous people involved with the Channel Tunnel could claim to have been the first to reconstitute the ancient link. Maybe the Frenchman and Englishman who completed the last metres of the tunnel, carrying their Tricolour and Union Jack, maybe those on the inaugural train journey in 1994. Possibly a tunnel meant only for trains is too restricting and we must wait for the proposed motorway tunnel to say that the old valley has truly been resurrected. Or perhaps the honour has already fallen to a Russian vagabond who in 1998 beat all manner of security cameras and anti-rabies barriers to sneak into the Folkestone entrance and walk the entire thirty miles to France. For almost three days he marched along the tracks, huddling against the wall as trains sped past and spending two nights asleep on the floor of passages leading to the service tunnel. He was lucky not to have been killed. But having left a Russian ship in Scotland, then made his way through the length of Britain without money, papers or any English, he was unlucky to have got no further than the French police who were waiting at their end of the tunnel. His dream? To join the Foreign Legion. Too old, they told him, and sent him straight back to England. Unsuccessful though he was, he had managed, by walking from England to France, to turn back the clocks by 8,000 years.

Hoping to see one of the famous cricket matches, I joined a hovercraft making a special trip out to the Goodwin Sands for the hours of low tide.

The day was unseasonally cold and wet, but that did not seem to discourage my fellow passengers, a baroque crowd including humourless bird-watchers in khaki, red-faced country people, pensioners with tartan rugs and wicker hampers, bearded men in sailor's caps, couples in black leather, the odd dandy in a Panama hat and an organ grinder named Busker John. On board the *Princess Margaret*, the captain advised that once we reached the sands we shouldn't stray too far from the waiting hovercraft and risk missing the trip back. When the sea came in, he warned, dry land turned to quicksand and pulled down anything or anyone on it. We were asked to synchronize our watches and shortly after the *Princess Margaret* came to rest. A strange, giddy atmosphere reigned as we walked down the rear ramp into the drizzle. We had two hours to play on eighteen square miles of dunes that shortly after our departure would disappear.

The Goodwins are perhaps the greatest shipping hazard in Europe, a submerged island in the nexus of the English Channel and North Sea, an even busier shipping lane than around the Scillies. And unlike the Scillies, this temporary land cannot be charted with accuracy, as the contours shift with every storm. Since the Middle Ages some 2,000 ships and many more small boats that went unrecorded have foundered there. Sailors called the Goodwins 'ships-swallower' and 'widow-maker'. Although their surface is as empty as the moon, underneath lies a city of bones and ships' carcasses. Maps showing the location of wrecks are sold on posters and tea towels, but there is not enough room to squeeze in all the names.

At the same time as we arrived, a large red cargo ship ploughed up the North Sea to our east. 'Look how far off she stays. They all stay that far off the Goodwins when the weather's poor,' said an old man in a white-topped yachting cap. 'You see, once you've grounded on the Goodwin Sands, you're unlikely ever to get off.'

Rocks may hole or shatter a hull in seconds, but the sands spin out their execution. The crew may be unharmed after the initial grounding and they may believe that the next rising tide will free their vessel, but it only loosens the hard surface and, as the waters continue to mount, the ship is forced inexorably into the ground. Trapped, she is then either battered to pieces by waves or gradually sucked out of sight.

Although tragedies of this sort took place within just a few miles of the Kent ports and the North Foreland lighthouse, the dangers of negotiating the sands in bad weather, especially in the days of oar and sail, often made rescue impossible. The Reverend T. Stanley Treanor, chaplain of the Missions of Seamen in the port of Deal, was delivering a sermon on a vessel about to sail to South Africa when he saw another ship vanish before the lifeboats could arrive. He wrote in 1888:

My eyes were riveted. There I saw, three miles off, our two lifeboats of Kingsdown and Walmer, each in tow of a steamer which came to their aid, making for the Goodwins, and on the outer edge of the Goodwins I beheld a hapless brig, with sails set, aground. I saw her at that distance lifted by the heavy sea, and at that distance I saw the great tumble of the billows. That she had heavily struck the bottom I also saw, for crash! – and even at that distance I verily seemed to hear the crash – away went her mainmast over her side, and the next instant she was gone, and had absolutely and entirely disappeared. I could not believe my eyes, and rubbed them and gazed again and yet again. She had perished with all hands. The lifeboats, fast as they went, were just too late, and found nothing but a nameless boat, bottom upwards, and a lifebelt, and no one ever knew her nationality or name.

The greatest single disaster on the Goodwins took place during a monstrous storm in late November 1703. What Daniel Defoe called 'this terrible blast' was said to have lifted men and animals through the air. All over England chimneys and roofs collapsed, killing many people in their homes. Near Bristol 15,000 sheep drowned. Off Plymouth, the recently built Eddystone lighthouse was obliterated, along with its architect Henry Winstanley. Caught right in this storm was a large naval fleet led by none other than Sir Cloudesley Shovel, the same admiral who would die, along with more than 1,600 of his men, four years later at the other end of the Channel.

Sir Cloudesley's fleet was in the Downs, the partially sheltered anchorage between the Goodwins and the Kent coast, when the storm struck. Some of his ships made miraculous escapes after their captains tore down their masts to reduce wind resistance and allowed the storm to carry them, out of control, as far as Holland and Norway. But four major fighting vessels, along with 1,190 men, did not survive the night. On the ships that sank, there were few survivors. The relatively small man-of-war *Mary* had a crew of 273, but only one man, the extraordinarily lucky Thomas Atkins, lived. He was first washed overboard, then a wave carried and threw him on to the deck of another vessel, the *Stirling Castle*. When this ship also ran aground, he again went overboard, but this time landed directly in a lifeboat. That, at least, is the story passed down.

An unusual victim added to the litany was the *South Goodwin* lightship, destroyed in 1954 by one of the very storms it was meant to warn against. Lightships have lamps but no motors and are anchored permanently in places where lighthouses cannot be built. Accidents were rare, but unlike the lighthouse keepers the crews of these floating lights (now automated, along with lighthouses) faced at least the possibility of sinking. The *South Goodwin* broke her moorings during a severe gale, also at the end of November, hit the sands and capsized. One man, a young ornithologist who'd come to study bird migration, was found clinging to the capsized hull, but the captain and crew of six were never seen again.

The strangeness of the Goodwins is that all this is invisible. Sand masks the destruction and the sea, twice every day, washes away the tears. The daily magic act of this offshore desert excited the Victorians, who started the tradition of cricket matches at low tide. On the day of my visit, though, the imagined tableau of whites, umpires and scoreboards rising out of the sea never materialized. The rain didn't help, but in any case my companions were either too anarchic or too pedestrian. The only attempt at a match was a half-hearted duel between a giant and his short-sighted son. Many, including myself, searched for some sign of the graveyard – a mast poking out or the sandy silhouette of a buried hull. Relics are sometimes found. The anchor of a French ship once yanked up the coffin of one Francis Merrydith, who had asked to be buried in the sands but, because of this disturbance, ended up in Hamburg. All we saw, however, were sand – hard sand, wet sand, flat sand and cratered sand – and, where the sand ended, water.

Others on the expedition came as colonizers, making themselves at home in these inhospitable and foreign surroundings. Hardy picknickers staked their claim with boiled eggs, coleslaw sandwiches, Colman's mustard, champagne and tea. The driving rain did not put them off. A lone Scotsman paraded his Maclean tartan kilt. 'I'm probably the first Scot to come to the sands since the devolution of Parliament, so that would make me the ambassador,' he said in an Essex accent. 'Actually, I just got the kilt through a relative who died. Seemed like an opportunity to give it an airing.' The ambassador's thin legs looked frozen. Another man brought suburbia in the shape of his mother and a set of golf clubs. He hit twelve balls into the desert and lost one. Soon, all these little kingdoms would be gone and the sea would rule again.

'It's strange,' said Busker John, the organ-grinder. 'People have always tried to avoid these sands like the plague and here we are paying to come. Gives me the creeps. The hairs stand up on my neck, they do.' But that didn't stop him doing a little jig in the middle of the sands and singing, 'Oh, I do like to be beside the seaside'. Busker John made the trip once a year. He was sixty-nine, and he wore a Breton sailor's cap, a black waistcoat, a white shirt and a red bandanna. One badge on his waistcoat displayed the Union Jack and read 'these colours don't run'. Another advertised the British Organ Grinders' Association.

With fifteen minutes to go before we had to be back on the hovercraft, I pulled my clothes off and ran into the sea. The current shook my body like a tambourine.

The big Channel chart was good for dreaming at my desk in London, but as soon as I was in Keyhaven it was my second purchase, Admiralty chart 2040, covering just the western Solent, 120 nautical miles west of the Goodwins, that had my attention.

On the main chart, scale 1:500,000, the western Solent was the size of my little finger and Keyhaven almost touched the Isle of Wight, but on chart 2040 the western Solent, scale 1:20,000, was bigger than my arm. I could almost pretend that I was looking at not only one section of one stretch of water, but an equal of the Channel itself, with mustard-yellow Hampshire being England and far-off Wight the northern part of France.

If nothing else, the chart helped me to realize that the place I'd chosen to learn to sail, however small, was a real and busy chunk of sea. Markings included a lighthouse at Hurst Castle;

54

underwater cables; a wreck; zones set aside for trawlers and for dredgers; dangerous banks that broke the surface at low tide; and, in purple, WARNING – LARGE VESSELS TURNING.

Of all the markings, one stood out: the tiny anchor symbol in Hurst Castle bay next to Keyhaven – an anchorage. When I'd bought *Aquila*, an anchor attached to two metres of chain and twenty-five metres of rope came as part of the gear, but at the time I'd barely expected to put it to use. Dinghies were always pulled up on beaches or trolleys, or tied to quays, but hardly ever anchored. That was something real boats did – boats that were not just runabouts, but small ships. I'd had no idea where one could, or was even allowed to, anchor, but the chart, with that anchor symbol, gave the answer. An idea entered my head: I'd learn to anchor and then, at least in some small way, *Aquila* would earn the dignity of a real ship.

In *Sailing: A Beginner's Guide*, the chapter 'Anchoring Under Sail' came well into the book. 'Anchoring takes time and effort, and no one will be too anxious to reanchor if the spot you've chosen isn't right,' it warned. According to the directions, I was to steer *Aquila* sharply into the wind until we'd stalled and the sails were flapping. Adèle would then crawl on to the bow and lower the anchor. The amount of line to be paid out depended on the depth, but a ratio of at least 3:1 was recommended to make sure the anchor took a firm grip; 5:1 was better. In the castle bay, where the depths did not exceed four metres, that meant putting out between twelve and twenty metres of line.

One May weekend, Adèle and I sailed out of Keyhaven into the bay and approached the area marked on the chart, a place where the shingle beach curved back on itself just before the entrance into the Solent. At a spot about fifteen or so metres off the beach, we went into action. For a second, the whole thing seemed ridiculously easy. The boat obeyed, we stalled, and Adèle edged up past the sails, the plough-shaped anchor, iron chain and length of rope in her hands. But as soon as she had gone beyond the point of no return, *Aquila*'s elegant pause in mid-water came to an end. The wind seized the sails and I was powerless to stop us flying off again. In self-preservation as much as anything else, Adèle, now clinging to the jib, let the anchor drop overboard. On we sailed, the line paid out and suddenly *Aquila* jerked to a halt. Our path looked nothing like the tidy progress of matchstick boats drawn in the sailing manual diagrams, but the end result was the same.

From now on, whenever we pushed off from Keyhaven, we carried the anchor. Not only the anchor, but food and sleeping bags, which we packed away into *Aquila*'s two lockers, or tied up under the benches. To others, we may have looked simply like another Wayfarer dinghy setting out for a couple of hours of sailing. But knowing that we would not come back that night gave me the secret pleasure, every time, of starting a new journey. However briefly, we were going to live on the sea.

The anchoring soon got better and although none of this directly affected sailing, each night on *Aquila* was a lesson. Learning every corner of that tiny space, becoming comfortable moving around on a pitching boat, even organizing the stowing of gear – all of this brought *Aquila* and me closer. Even if I still had a long way to go in learning to sail, anchoring opened a new world. It was as if by being anchored, by cutting dependence on land, *Aquila* instantly became more than a dinghy and I more than a day-sailor.

Bed was on the floor, which was small and cluttered, but just long and wide enough for a sleeping bag and an inflatable mattress on each side of the centreboard case. By tying a canvas cover down over the boom we got a good tent-like roof, while cooking took place on a camping stove placed on the floor in the stern. Conditions were actually far better than usual when camping. Good food could be brought without worry, weight was much less of a problem and there was no dirt. Rather than having to carry our camp, the camp carried us.

When the early summer nights floated in, even the birds fell silent, except for the occasional secret beat of a wing over the mast. The moon turned the darkened parapets of Hurst Castle into a camel train. The water moved, flooding and ebbing in gigantic, slow-motion breaths, the currents bowling tiny bubbles of phosphorescence under the hull. Lying down, less than a centimetre of fibreglass separated our heads from the sea, while above, only the canvas tent kept us from the sky and the blink of the lighthouse at the edge of the Trap. Boats at anchor naturally face into the wind and when the wind shifts direction, they too swing across the water. The effect, as *Aquila* swung left to right to left to right, was to send the stars spinning until I felt dizzy.

Gently caressed by red wine and cradled in the arms of the sea, I liked to lie back and dream. I dreamed of the next day when I would haul up the sails, reattach the rudder, raise the anchor and move off into the wind, without ever having to put a foot on land. I dreamed of reaching the Isle of Wight, of sailing out of the Solent and into the real Channel; of sailing until I found a place I'd never been; of losing sight of land; of passing ocean-going ships, a blip in their wake; of landing in

France, where the local people would not believe I'd left from England. All of this seemed possible, for in every minute that I stared up into the sky, the constellations pouring past, we travelled a million miles or more. Possible, at least until dawn, when the birds woke, not with the warbling of gardens, but with the austere shrieks and laments of the sea.

Other boats, though never other dinghies, often anchored by the castle in the summer months. Most were yachts sailed by retirees. It seemed that only they could afford the life. Some looked with pity on our tiny craft, others with derision, but we paid them little attention. Their boats seemed to have been named after holiday bungalows – *Melody*, *Sweetness*, *Aurora*. Other sailors made us admiring salutes, remembering, perhaps, their own early days afloat, and with these we often made friends, chatting a little over the gunwales, offering each other news and advice. It didn't take long before Adèle and I felt that *Aquila* truly belonged.

The busiest time in the bay was in late afternoon as yachts returned for the night. In they motored, sails lowered, circling about looking for the right spot before dropping anchor with a feverish rattle of chain. By evening, the result was a floating village, a mini-community where we were all self-contained but shared the same space and were obliged, by both custom and maritime law, to help each other when in distress. The names and nature of each yacht quickly became as familiar as the landscape of any home neighbourhood. Music might seep from one, laughter or the smell of cooking from another. There always seemed to be one crew having trouble anchoring and one yacht more handsome than all the rest. Different from being on land, though, was that in the morning, with the sun and rising breeze, this village would disintegrate, each home disappearing out to sea. There were never long goodbyes, a wave at most. Sometimes a boat set out early and one woke to find empty water in the place occupied by the friendly neighbour of the night before. By the next evening another village, rarely with the same boats or characters, would have formed.

This was the way, we were learning, of all harbours. Sailors were quick to meet and quick to leave, fluid as the tide. Yet there was always a sensation that we'd meet again. Sailing boats move slowly and they are ruled by the weather, meaning that their range is usually quite limited. And because every boat has its own character, they are easy to recognize and their owners with them. The morning farewell, then, was quite different from the goodbye one might say after a chance meeting on a train. The sea separated, but also bound all of us afloat.

I took to this world from the start. Indeed, it could almost have been designed for me, for throughout my life I'd had the disadvantage, or maybe advantage, of not being able to call any land my own. I had an American passport, but I was a British resident, had lived in Britain most of my life and spoke like an Englishman. With a name like Smith, most people assumed that I was. However, I'd been born in Spain and one of my two middle names was Manuel, in honour of my godfather. My other middle name was von Bormann, my mother's maiden name. Not that she was really a German – that would have been too easy – for my grandfather was Russian and his wife, my grandmother, came from a family that was Germanized but originally French. The United States would have been the perfect place for me, obviously, but I was not fated to live there, so when I went on visits to see

American uncles or cousins, I still remained an outsider. With my accent, no one believed that I was American at all. For so many years, I'd secretly dreaded that question: 'Where are you from?'

Now, on the sea, my boat was my home and the anchorage my country. After all, that was all that people cared about out there. When they asked, 'Where are you from?' they were referring to the last port of call. Even if someone on shore asked me where I was from, or whether I was a local or just visiting, I had an answer which, for the first time in my life, felt whole: 'I'm sailing. That's my boat, the small one, *Aquila*.' It was ironic. For years I'd dreamed of putting down roots, but it was here on the surface of the water, where roots could not grow, that I felt suddenly at home.

One night, we made friends with a couple who anchored near us. Their yacht was about twenty-five feet long and shaped like an oversized American Indian canoe. It had once been a launch on a navy ship. She had no name and this couple were trying her out before buying. I liked them. Unlike many of the other yachties, they weren't dressed as if they'd just stepped from a chandler's and their boat hadn't been made to look like a suburban living room on water. They were anchored about fifteen metres from us, which was close enough to talk and far enough to keep our privacy. Each time we swung on our anchor line so did our neighbours and therefore the distance between us changed little.

Why were they thinking of buying? I asked. 'To get out there and have an adventure,' the man said, grinning. 'The advantage of this boat is that she has a retractable keel, so we can go in shallow waters and go aground at low tide. The disadvantage is that with such a light keel we can be easily overpowered – like a dinghy.' He was nimble around the boat and did everything with a quick, strong hand. The next morning, there were gentle breezes under a clear sky. We were invited to come over and have coffee, but we told them we'd already brewed some on our camping stove and they gave us a thumb's-up. When they hauled up their anchor and left, I shouted 'Good adventures,' and I meant it.

Adèle and I managed to get down from London together every weekend and every free day. We were learning rapidly now. It wasn't just that we'd had the basics from Jim or that I was reading all the instruction books I could find. Somehow *Aquila* urged us on. She was a beauty, but she was also bursting with power – underused power. I knew, looking at that sharp, strong bow, sturdy rudder and polished gunwales, that this boat was not only able but willing to take us far. She was a courageous boat and courage, like fear, is infectious.

We'd always set off from Keyhaven, whatever the weather, with the mainsail reefed to half its full size. No precaution seemed too much, for however small the western Solent was in reality, the view from Keyhaven looked gigantic. Immediately to the west was the gap between Hurst Castle and Wight – the Trap – which would take us out into the open sea but remained off limits because of the notorious currents. To the south was the Isle of Wight, close enough for us to see the woods and cliffs, but somehow terrifyingly distant. And eastwards, the water seemed to go on for ever. Somewhere out there was Southampton and Cowes. I wondered if I'd ever get that far; after all, we'd not even been to Lymington, the harbour just two miles away on the Hampshire coast, let alone to Yarmouth on the Isle of Wight.

One June day, though, the idea of reefing back seemed just too ridiculous. It was a calm day and other dinghies swept past with full sails, even spinnakers, which are made from the lightest of materials to catch every breath of wind and balloon out from the front of the boat. Emboldened by our latest overnight stay, we decided the time had come to handle bigger sails. So we pulled *Aquila* up on the beach and dismantled the reefing that we'd so laboriously tied down, then pulled up the main. This was a bit like taking the stabilizers off a child's bicycle and I had to keep telling myself that we were doing the right thing.

With that, we sailed out of the bay and into the Solent. As always, we started with the intention of turning around at some invisible line and heading back. Like fish meeting the walls of a glass tank, we'd never gone outside these self-imposed limits that lay maybe fifteen or twenty minutes' sail in each direction. Now, however, we reached the usual line, crossed and kept going. We were aiming straight at the Isle of Wight. There was no decision and no announcement, just a feeling that something had changed. At a turbulent patch of water in mid-Solent, we simply kept going. The ride got a little bumpy, but nothing more. Adèle and I looked at each other and laughed, not daring to speak. We were on course for Wight. Twenty minutes later, we'd arrived.

The place where we landed was a shingle beach at Fort Victoria. It was rather steep and *Aquila* was heavy to pull, but we managed to get her halfway out of the water, then in celebratory mood strolled up to a café for brunch. I felt the exhilaration of having arrived after a voyage. The bacon, eggs, toast and large pot of tea were going to taste good, no doubt even better than the same food ordered by people at the other tables. They had arrived by cars and buses, but we had arrived by sea. I looked proudly over to *Aquila*.

Disaster! The boat we'd left one minute before on the shingle had somehow slipped backwards and was now about to float into the sea. I hadn't noticed any waves while we were landing, but they were there now and were literally washing *Aquila* away. The waves, I realized, were from the wake of powerboats and ships steaming past the beach on their way through the Trap. Each wave seemed to gather force as it broke on the beach, loosening the shingle every time and sucking *Aquila* a little further back. Very soon, she'd be away. Trying not to attract attention, I put down my fork and walked slowly back along the beach. Another series of waves struck. *Aquila* bounced and swung with a grinding noise on the shingle. I walked quicker. More waves. I ran.

After hauling *Aquila* back as high up the beach as I could, I returned to Adèle and our table. The eggs had gone cold, but the tea was still hot. 'No problem, it's nothing,' I began to say. Another series of waves washed in. This beach was a wave magnet and *Aquila* was unhappy. In fact she was being battered and tossed worse than before. Now a wave broke against her low stern and washed into the boat. The fork in my hand felt suddenly heavy and my appetite was gone. 'Let's get out of here,' I said. Now not caring who watched, or what they thought, we ran back down the beach, pushed *Aquila* into the water, jumped aboard and returned to Keyhaven, humbled.

For several weeks, the pattern was unchanged. Every step of progress came paired with at least one bad stumble. Whenever we thought we'd mastered some matter, the sea interrupted, changing the rules by the day.

Once, we stopped for lunch in Hurst Castle bay. There,

the beach was properly sheltered and on a gradual incline, so there'd be no worries about waves. We pulled *Aquila* half out of the water and hiked off to sit by an old tar-covered fisherman's hut along the beach. Nothing could have been easier. But when we got back a couple of hours later, the tide had ebbed so rapidly that *Aquila* now sat several metres from the water's edge, too far to drag without damaging her hull. We'd simply forgotten the speed at which the tide dropped. There was nothing to do except wait hours, feeling foolish, for the sea to rise again. On another occasion, when we'd just made our longest sail to date, we returned triumphantly to Keyhaven only to discover that sailing the last 500 metres through the marshes against the current was impossible in such light winds. We tried repeatedly, but kept getting pushed to one side, or backwards. The light faded, both of us became exasperated and finally *Aquila* ran aground on the mud. When a motorized dinghy from a yacht passed, we enthusiastically accepted the offer of a tow, something that would have seemed inconceivable in the flush of success an hour before.

These were simple, minor hiccups, but in essence the same lesson learned by every sailor, whether in Keyhaven or mid-Atlantic: that the sea is a living, moving thing and therefore unpredictable. Another lesson, this one peculiar to those crossing the Channel, was that this sea might be narrow, but the path across was long. That distance was relative entirely to the man and machine would be true anywhere, but on the sea, with its moods and strength, even more so. Twenty-two miles at the narrowest point didn't sound like much, but that distance had been enough to stop many in their tracks. At sea, even one mile might easily turn out to be too far. And this applied not only to those in the swirling waters but also to those above. I had only to think of the Blériot family to know that.

When Louis Blériot, a dashing Frenchman with sorrowful eyes and a vast moustache, flew across the Channel in 1909, it was akin to the moon landing of his day. The only other men to have gone by air were the balloonists Pierre Blanchard, who also invented the parachute, and Boston doctor John Jeffries, who floated over in 1784.

Blériot made his conquest with the insouciance of an amateur. The story was that a white horse towed his frail plane to the take-off field and then, after cattle had been cleared, the Frenchman simply asked, 'Which way to Dover?' and took to the air. Over the Channel, where his English rival Hubert Latham had ditched just six days before, Blériot became disoriented. 'I have passed the destroyer and I turn my head to see whether I am proceeding in the right direction. I am amazed. There is nothing to see, neither the torpedo-destroyer, nor France, nor England. I can see nothing at all – *rien du tout!* It is a strange position, to be alone, unguided, without compass, in the air of the middle of the Channel,' he told a reporter after landing. 'I touch nothing. My hands and feet rest lightly on the levers. I let the aeroplane take its own course. I care not whither it goes. For ten minutes I continue, neither rising, nor falling, nor turning.' Shortly after, he saw Dover and was able, but only just, to coax his underpowered machine over the cliffs and into a rough landing behind the castle. One of the first at the scene, an English policeman, greeted Blériot with a kiss on the cheeks.

Just a year before I'd started to sail, the grandson of Blériot had attempted a re-enactment of the historic flight. The grandson was not flying the original plane, but one of the same vintage and model, and his name was identical: Louis Blériot. If all went well, he'd follow the same route, taking off from Calais and landing shortly after in a field near Dover Castle.

Hoping to witness the event, I'd got up before dawn at the King's Head Arms, a crooked old pub on the beach in Deal, and taken a taxi out along the road to Dover. It had been difficult to get information, apparently because the rights to the story were held exclusively by a French documentary film company and the *Daily Mail*, which had sponsored the original flight in 1909. All I'd managed to gather were the approximate time and place: early in the morning, somewhere on the Deal side of Dover.

The rising sun sharpened my senses. Even the taxi driver seemed caught up in the chase as we wound along the coastal road searching for a likely field. Suddenly the bulk of Dover Castle loomed. We were almost in the town and I was wondering if we'd have to turn back. Just then we saw a small group of tired-looking people and a few cars parked on the verge. The field didn't seem especially flat and there were no markings to suggest that it would soon be a runway, but this had to be it. I got out of the taxi and approached the group. 'Is this where Monsieur Blériot will be landing?' They didn't have to answer; the look of annoyance confirmed I was right.

The weather was perfect that day, with light winds and clear skies, yet the morning slipped away without a sign of the plane. The *Daily Mail* reporters, po-faced, nondescript men, talked anxiously. The French film crew, its producer a nervous Paul McCartney lookalike, paced up and down. Someone came over to tell us that there had been a delay. Meanwhile, the little huddle of people grew.

By mid-morning it was obvious that something had gone

wrong. The spectators – me, a man whose father had seen the first Blériot land in 1909, a moustachioed old fellow with giant sideburns and a gold-buttoned blazer, and a few weary locals – peered into the sky, but we should have been watching the film crew; they were packing up. 'It's not going to happen,' Paul McCartney said with a final suspicious glance at my notebook, as if I might have been the cause of his problems. 'He couldn't take off. There won't be any flight.' Everyone reacted differently to the news. I slumped as the lack of sleep finally caught up; the French looked peeved; the *Mail* men talked grimly into mobile phones; the man with the blazer held forth on the problems of aeronautics.

As I later discovered, Blériot did take off, but he never made it even as far as the coast, crashing instead into a lake near Calais. Maybe he'd courted bad luck by wearing a wet suit for the flight. Maybe his plane was jinxed. Ten years before, an Englishwoman had tried to make her own crossing in that very aircraft and had crashed in the Channel just short of Dover. The plane was a sort of flying dinghy, a flimsy contraption of canvas wings, wooden framework body and single engine with a wooden propeller. Because ailerons had not been invented by 1909, steering was carried out by pulling on wires to change the shape of the wings, like a sail. At least Blériot's failure was authentic, for nothing had been upgraded to make the journey easier or safer. In fact, what was surprising was not Blériot Junior's failure but his grandfather's success. Now the pilot of my own fragile machine, I could only think of the Blériot family with admiration.

Anchored in Hurst Castle bay one morning, I'd just woken and was contemplating leaving the cocoon of my sleeping bag when I heard a muffled shout, 'Hello, *Aquila*! Hello, *Aquila*! Sebastian, hello there!' I started. I'd not slept well. It had been our first night anchored in strong winds, with *Aquila* swinging on her anchor line like a drunk around a lamppost. The rigging howled all night and Adèle and I'd kept wondering whether the anchor would hold and, if not, how we'd stop ourselves drifting away in the dark. Over at the castle, more forbidding than ever, I'd seen lights flicker by the water's edge late into the night. No one lived there, so who had it been? The lights were probably just from night fishermen, but my sleep was disturbed by dreams of smugglers and killers. Now, barely audible through the wind, someone was calling my name. I broke free of my sleeping bag, pulled back the cover from the boom and blinked. The water was grey under an overcast sky and wind pockmarked the surface. Flecks of spray struck my face. Another dinghy, a Wayfarer with two people in it, was close by.

'Sebastian, is that you? It's Rob – from Oxford.'

'My God, it's you. I can't believe it,' I replied. This was the man who only two months before had sold me *Aquila*.

'We've been cruising. We spent the night here in the bay last night – further up there. We didn't see you anchored here,' he said.

'No, I didn't see you either. Where are you going now?'

'We're going to try to go on to Lymington, but with this wind and that messy sea out there, I'm not so sure,' he said. 'Well done for camping like that. I'm impressed. Well, here we go. Bye there. You'd better not go out in the Solent today. Stay in the bay.' So saying, Rob and his Wayfarer companion set off, mainsail reefed right down, jib furled altogether, and disappeared into the Solent.

Rob, I remembered, was one of those people who are competent at almost any practical matter. Ask him to tie a knot, build a table, fix a car or wire a house – he could probably do it in his sleep. Even the way he'd sailed by us that morning and then gone out into the Solent had the stamp of clinical precision. So I admired, but envied him. The day I'd bought *Aquila* I'd tried to disguise the fact that I was a novice, but I'd never known for sure whether the bluff had worked or not. Now I knew. The fact that he'd seen me camping in the bay on such a night was in my favour. He even seemed genuinely impressed. But there had been that fatal last phrase: 'You'd better not go out in the Solent today.' And then, as if to show the difference between us, he'd immediately gone out himself.

To my delight, not five minutes passed before Rob's Wayfarer reappeared in the bay. He and his companion had decided not to fight the storm all the way down the Solent to Lymington after all. They were soaked and, maybe I was imagining it, looked rather haggard. I chuckled. So pleased was I at their retreat that I failed to notice the rudder of *Aquila*, which I'd not properly secured, being lifted from her fitting by a small wave.

'God, the rudder,' shouted Adèle. In her French accent and still incomplete grasp of English nautical vocabulary, what I heard was, 'God, the radar.'

'The radar?'

Adèle was very excited now. 'Yes, look, the radar is flying away!'

I wasn't mystified for long. There was the rudder, floating rapidly through the choppy water across the bay. Without the rudder, the boat was crippled. I felt a sudden chill.

I started to strip to swim, but Rob had already got there, expertly braking his boat long enough for his companion to reach down and pluck the rudder out of the water. Then, defying the violent wind, he performed the same neat pause next to *Aquila* and passed us our runaway goods. 'You'd better look after that,' he said. We thanked him profusely, but inside my humiliation was complete. 'We'll see you back in Keyhaven. Don't go out there,' he said, and roared off. The way he pronounced 'out there', the bay could have been a bunker and the Solent a street under heavy bombardment. More or less simultaneously, Adèle and I said, 'Let's go.'

Mimicking what we'd seen, we left off the jib and hauled up only the deep-reefed main. Out we went. The Solent was indeed wickedly rough. The sea ran and boiled. Water splashed heavily into the boat and on to our oilskins, but on we went. To my surprise, nothing could have felt better. We made several runs out towards Wight and back. In one direction, the waves broke on *Aquila*'s bow and in the other they welled up alarmingly high behind, then slipped harmlessly under the stern. We were nervous and never quite sure whether we were really in control, but *Aquila* seemed to be in her element. I remembered the words of The Major: 'A good sea boat.' That's right, I thought, a good sea boat, and that's why I am going to make it across the English Channel after all.

Our clumsiness in *Aquila* faded imperceptibly as the summer wore on until the basic tasks that had once seemed so difficult became second nature. With increased control, our focus broadened from worrying over some particular rope or pulley to learning to feel the sea, the waves and the wind. The scope of our trips also increased. Most of the western Solent was beginning to fall within range and we no longer felt obliged to spend nights at the castle. These advances did not mean that we no longer ran into trouble on occasion, only that we'd started to see these mishaps more like lessons than misfortune.

Beginner's Guide in hand, we might practise tacking one day, docking another. We might work on estimating wind speeds, then experiment by making the sails slightly larger, or we might simply learn knots, or read and re-read all the complicated sections on trimming sails and finding the perfect balance. Not everything made sense yet, but enough to give almost everything a try. So it was, with apprehension, but knowing that at some point I must begin, that I took my first steps sailing single-handed.

Aquila seemed to be designed for two and after my first sortie alone I returned shaken. Adèle was slight and light, but without her added kilos to help create balance, *Aquila* felt like a nervous horse on oats. The boat heeled over more quickly and violently, the sails pulled with what felt like twice the power and my two hands never seemed sufficient. Tacking was a roulette that I won only occasionally. Too often when I turned through the wind, I'd manage to keep hold of the mainsail controls but lose my grip on the tiller. Or I'd get my feet tangled in some rope. Or I'd forget altogether to release the jib controls to allow the sail to swing over to the other side. In that hour, I'd entered a hole where I felt the first, light drops of fear.

Gradually, though, I began to take control. As my sailing books told me, I needed to reef the sail deeper and earlier when alone, and I had to sharpen all my decision-making and reactions. In tacking, I could not afford to lose a second when

I switched sides. The movement had to be absolutely in rhythm with the boat as her deck swung from one angle to another. Dealing with the mainsail and jib simultaneously was also a question of timing and rhythm, and gradually I found I could begin to manoeuvre *Aquila* in any direction. I felt almost as if I were having to learn from the start all over again and in a way I was, for these were the small beginnings of an entirely new stage. I was enthralled. I'd always seen *Aquila* as a tool for me to enter the watery world, but not until these outings alone did I begin to understand that eventually she might become much more: she could be my partner.

2

I n midsummer, I decided on a trip along the south coast by car, ending in Dover, where I would take the ferry to meet Adèle in Calais. It would do me good, I thought, not only to take a break from *Aquila* but to escape the microcosm of the Solent. After all, I'd set out to explore the whole Channel, yet because of the sailing had barely gone ten miles in any direction. I wanted to get a feel for the rest of this sea.

My run began in Bognor Regis. Passing through the resort, I thought of King George V's dying words, or at least his famously reported words, and could only agree. 'Bugger Bognor!' indeed. Maybe it was my mood, my hangover or a muggy sun, but the sea front seemed joyless: underfed teenage girls, hair gelled and pinned over pale faces; prowling men with shaved heads and tattoos; women shouting at mobile phones; an overweight family feeding at the candyfloss stand. People must have been having fun but it was hard to tell. Even the sea, flattened by the breathless heat, was uninviting. To swim would be like climbing into wet sheets. I continued east without pause, stopping only when I realized, quite suddenly, that I'd reached Brighton.

I sensed in Brighton the mysterious, escapist power of the Channel. Once this had been a sea of real escapees – the Channel of fleeing Huguenots and French aristocrats, of Oscar Wilde, of Byron and Byron's creation Childe Harold, of Horatio Nelson's bankrupt mistress Emma Hamilton, even of

Lord Lucan on the Newhaven–Dieppe ferry in 1974. For them, the Channel marked a frontier, a Rio Grande of the north, and although that seemed passé in the days of European integration and world travel, the Channel hadn't lost its fundamental pull. Here was a sea where on some days you saw the other side and on others you did not. These waters contained all the promise of a new start. That was why it seemed to me that even for ordinary people there was some extra dimension to the Channel 'pleasure resorts' that other coasts did not have. Somehow being on the south coast, on the sea closest to France, the gateway to Europe, brought energy and optimism. Even the weather was supposedly better here, although that wasn't always evident, than in the rest of Britain. People dared plant palm trees!

Brighton was definitely a bolt hole, even if in a very particular way. While other south coast resorts had once been popular for cures – Hastings for chest weakness and rheumatism, the chalky water on the Kent coast for soft bones, Southampton for gout, Bournemouth for lung ailments – Brighton had, since the arrival of the Prince Regent in the 1780s, been the home of hedonists and illicit lovers. I wasn't after the town's 'dirty weekends', but I did want a place with so much distraction and noise that I could spend my first evening alone on the road without having to hear myself think. In front of me the Palace Pier reared up, garish splendour against a sober evening sea, and for the first time that day I felt at ease.

At the Kimberley Hotel, the receptionist scrutinized me carefully when I asked for a room for one. It happened that, as I entered, a young woman had got out of her car, which was parked by the front door. The receptionist saw this, then took her conclusion too far, believing that I also had got out of that car. 'You sure you want a room for one?' I nodded. 'So she's not anything to do with you?' I shook my head. Thereupon, the receptionist remained exceptionally vigilant, suspicious of my notebook and mystified about why I was alone. I enjoyed that. Brighton, like the Regent's crazy pavilion, was a place of deceptions and fantasy, a crossing point, a town where the population was temporary and usual morals could be put on hold. So a few misunderstandings could be part of the game.

A heady atmosphere pulled me down through the small back streets to the sea front. The annual gay parade had taken place recently and there were still posters up. I wondered if 'Cirque du Pink, the UK's first and only gay circus' had done well. The closer I got to the sea, the lighter I felt. When I finally reached the promenade and the broad shingle beach, I breathed deeply. Because it was dark, I could only hear the sea and make out the lights of ships in the Channel. Nearby was the Palace Pier and beyond that the West Pier, ablaze with light bulbs. The iron legs under the Palace Pier looked so dainty I thought the whole structure would collapse as soon as it realized how flimsy it was.

That weakness, like so much else in Brighton, was an illusion. Piers started to be built around Britain in the early nineteenth century as somewhere for holiday-makers to disembark from steam ships, but it was when train travel put an end to that role that these strange structures really came into their own. Stripped of any function, the pier became something almost mystical, a symbol of the seaside holiday and all the freedoms that entailed. For the nineteenth-century family on holiday, the path led straight from the railway station to the promenade and from there to the pier, that light and fantastic structure which carried the ordinary man just a little bit further out to sea. Crowded with games, tricks and exotic architecture, the pier was a sort of micro-state in permanent suspension of disbelief, the illusion of a bridge, because it led only to itself.

Soon I was close enough to hear the Tannoy: 'When it comes to fun, everyone's a winner on the Brighton pier.' Music took over, something by Queen blaring out. I paused in the entrance, then the crowd swept me up and carried me through on to the main deck. All alone in a place where almost everyone seemed to be part of a group, I felt detached, almost as if I was watching through a lens. Teenagers roamed in search of mates, the girls dressed like the All Saints, their tight bellies on display, the lads in outfits of puritanical simplicity and muted aggression. Pensioners in macs and woolly hats sat on benches under ornate shelters as if waiting for the bus. A blonde, long-legged girl in a short skirt passed. I guessed at once she was Russian and I was right. A red-faced man said, 'Beautiful legs, darling,' and she, without breaking stride, replied, '*Poshol*,' a Russian abbreviation for 'Go fuck yourself.' Everyone else looked the way I felt: dazzled by the booming music, flashing lights and promises of happiness. In one corner was Gypsy Jim, the 'Acclaimed Aussie Palmist and Hypnotist', in another 'Taj Mahal Kebab'. I missed both and instead went straight into the Pleasure Dome. This turned out to be an electronic games hall, an inferno of machine guns, racing engines and shouting robots. I walked on to the end of the pier. Beyond a dark doorway, someone was singing Elvis. I entered. It was Elvis.

A youngish man on a stage was singing 'You Ain't Nothing but a Hound Dog'. He wore a tight red costume, giant sunglasses and a gold cape. A lot of people were standing around the stage drinking. A girl in front of me with red hair and high cheekbones danced slowly, hips swaying like sea grass in a current. She turned round and said, 'He's good, isn't he? You'd almost think he was real.' Elvis was followed by the All Saints girls, or rather three teenagers who looked like the All Saints and sounded pretty much the same. I felt numb. The impersonators, the drink, my tiredness, just the fact that I was out at the end of this pier with the sea moving below – I hardly knew who I was or what I was doing. The redhead kept smiling and swaying. Time to get out.

In the morning, the fine weather had gone. A dark sky hovered like a hammer. Nevertheless, the Palace Pier was already open, and not only open but booming and flashing as hard as the night before. The Tannoy made the same promise. Along the beach, the West Pier gave me a fright. The fairy creation of the night was a hideous, blackened mess in daylight. This had once been the main pier in Brighton, but it fell apart in the 1970s and had been closed ever since. At night, only the skeleton was lit up, for that was all that remained. Repairs were under way, but nothing could have looked more of a ruin. The West Pier cried out for the darkness.

In Eastbourne, I arrived just in time for the afternoon performance of the Honourable Artillery Company band on the promenade. That evening there would be *Scissor Happy* with Lionel Blair and a concert of 'light classics', but in the afternoons nothing could top the Honourable Artillery Company. Despite the drizzle, an audience of about 150, nearly all of them old men or old dears with permed white hair and large handbags, sat in a semicircle of deck chairs, buzzing with excitement. The bandstand was open-air but had ingenious sliding doors that could be positioned to protect the sheet music from the wind. The band sported red coats with gold braid and the odd medal. Their black trousers had red stripes down the side and the peaks of their caps glistened. They played trumpets, trombones, tubas and timpani, and between numbers stood to attention while the director, in white gloves and red sash, saluted us.

We had several marches, a waltz, a 'selection of Mancini magic', 'Royal Celebrations', 'The Typewriter'. Occasionally the director would throw out a comment, like, 'That was the signature tune for a radio detective series. Radio was good, wasn't it? I still think it's the best.' Or, 'Now we're going to take you back in time to the age of steam trains and oh how wonderful that was. I remember it well as a young boy, the excitement of going on holiday. The smell of steam – that really made the holiday.' Each time, he was warmly applauded. The concert ended, as every concert every day ended, with the regimental march and the national anthem.

Lolling in my blue and white deck chair, I tried to square this vision of the seaside with Brighton's bright lights, DJs, gay parade, teeming youth, nudist beach . . . That had been the escapist Channel, the one I thought I knew, but here was another, and one that was probably no less common: the Channel fortress, the thin line separating England from malign foreign influences. There were plenty of people here who'd never gone further south and wouldn't want to, or people who'd tried 'abroad' only to realize that the roast lamb, potatoes and gravy of the tattered Eastbourne hotels were better after all. People still talked about 'overseas' here. For them, there'd been no Channel Tunnel.

Maybe such different versions of the same coast, one right along from the other, were not all that surprising, for the Channel was only a reflection of England's contradictions: one Channel to embrace the world, the other to keep it out. There couldn't have been a more perfect symbol of this strange mix than at the nudist camp where I'd stopped off that morning, just out of curiosity, in the hills between Brighton and Eastbourne. The club comprised a field, a garden and a small bungalow that had once been a Cold War listening post. NATURISTS MAY BE SEEN BEYOND THIS POINT warned a notice on the wooden gate outside, but thankfully the weather was such that I found everybody dressed. John, who ran the camp, introduced me to his wife, Pam, and a bedraggled woman who appeared from a caravan. We drank tea and I asked whether being on the Channel made it easier to let go of inhibitions.

'There's a lot of naturism on the south coast,' John said, insisting on the term naturist rather than nudist, 'here, then down in Brighton, Fairlight, Birling Gap. Most of us are English, but being on the south coast you get a lot of Dutch and Germans. Obviously, it first came from there, from across the Channel. English people go over and see it without meaning to – it's everywhere over there. Then they think, Well, sod it, I'll try. The thing is, once you've done it, you just don't want the wet swimming costume any more.' Then again, added Pam, 'there're people who when they're abroad wouldn't dream of going anywhere but a naturist beach, yet as soon as they get back this side of the Channel they won't do it. In England, we're still basically prudes.' I could hardly think of John and Pam as prudes, but it was true that apart from their liking for undressing, they could have fitted in with ease down at Eastbourne. There were no orgies at the sun club, only nude spaghetti evenings and cook-outs on the lawn. The photo album I was allowed to flick through showed a variety of odd-shaped naked men and women barbecuing or playing mini-snooker, darts and board games. Not a hint of Saturnalia. So although being on England's southern sea did apparently help loosen things up, it was a very English kind of looseness – a bit like Brighton and Eastbourne combined into one.

What about a plan I'd read about in the local paper for nude nights at the Hastings Tesco? 'The Tesco story, it never got going,' John said. 'I'm not sure it was even really naturists who applied. It might have been some kind of prank.' He looked serious. 'You see, there are what I'd call real naturists and then there are those types who belong to, well, clubs.' The clubs John meant were bath and Jacuzzi houses where people might have anonymous sex. They were the *nudists*. Nudists were militant undressers, with their own magazine, *Starkers*, published in Bournemouth and a mission to overturn the more genteel and regulated world of naturism. Nudists sounded a lot seedier than naturists, but in theory at least maybe they were closer to the open, liberated version of the English Channel, shock troops of a Channel that opened England to the world. But I wouldn't have argued that with John, for he felt strongly about the issue. 'You read some of the ads in the local paper and sometimes you wonder what the world is coming to,' he said.

Actually, being racy or staid was only a matter of image, but beneath the gloss I soon discovered another type of resort, more like the seaside of Graham Greene's *Brighton Rock* than of postcards and popular myth. In *Brighton Rock*, the trappings of innocent pleasure – promenades, piers, music, sunbathing – are all there, but they disguise a seedy, threatening world where the seaside feels more like a trap than an escape. You get 'The Boy' hoping to save himself by killing Rose on the cliffs; Hale being knifed by the pier; Spicer dying in a boarding house; the bent lawyer, Mr Prewitt, being arrested as he tries to flee the country by ferry.

Today, those stories were repeated all the time. The fairground and gutter were still not separated by much. When I thought back, for all the neon signs, garlands of coloured bulbs and shop windows, Brighton had plenty of dark spaces, dark as the bruised eyes of the man I'd found staring at me at night through the glass of an adjacent telephone booth. Even in Eastbourne, with its tea rooms and genteel pleasures, there was a whiff of failure, of chipboard over windows and urine in bus stops. In Hastings, the whiff became a stench. '1066 Country', the signs said, but John Evans, director of a centre for the homeless there, described instead a demi-monde of squatters, drug addicts and all those miserable people who thought the sea would be the start, but discovered it was the end.

'Seaside towns everywhere suffer, but it's especially bad on the south coast,' Evans told me. 'They come from everywhere – Ireland, Scotland, the north-east, the north-west, the Midlands. Some are just looking for a life, some have been driven out because of things they got up to, some just want to get away, as far as possible, and they have some happier childhood memory of the seaside. They work their way south, trying to find Utopia, and they get all the way here and still don't find it. But by then they've run out of strength, so they never leave.' Many ended in Hastings because its empty, crumbling hotels and B&Bs were the perfect dumping ground for the homeless and sick not wanted by councils inland. The local morgue and hospitals were busy with an unusually high suicide rate among young men and cases of what was termed 'deliberate harm'. Hastings, where the train station was a minute's walk from the sea, was literally the end of the line.

Purely for suicides, the blinding white cliffs of Beachy Head, curving like wings along the sea, outdid Hastings, or anywhere else for that matter. The previous year there'd been twenty-eight suicides and at the telephone box near the top there was a board showing the Samaritans' twenty-four-hour number. Below the cliffs, just out to sea, stood a red and white striped lighthouse where keepers had once dreaded being posted. Eddie Mathews had told me of a young keeper, brand new to the service, who found the body of a woman among the rocks when he was crossing to land at low tide, then the body of a man when he returned at the next low tide, twelve hours later. This was one of the first towers to be automated.

On the day of my walk, I couldn't help looking around and wondering whether perhaps someone would jump that very afternoon. Nearly all suicides jump alone, they said in the coroner's office, although a few drive over and many years back an old couple leapt holding hands. But when I looked for people alone, I realized that I was the only one, and that other couples and families might in fact be looking at me. I crawled to the edge and took a photograph, 180 metres up above the milky lips of the chalk-bottomed sea. Maybe this was the spot where Jimmy, the young Mod, rode his moped over in the final scene of the film *Quadrophenia*. The film was shot on a sunny day and in those conditions the white cliff sides and the Channel surface shone like another world. Jimmy's fatal flight really felt like freedom.

Not shown in the film, though, was the plaque on a granite stone set into the ground about twenty metres from the edge:

> Mightier
> than the thunders
> of many waters,
> mightier
> than the waves
> of the sea,
> the Lord high
> is mighty!
>   Psalm 93:4
>
> God is always greater
> than all of our troubles.

While on the road, as if to compensate for my absence from *Aquila*, I constantly gravitated to water and boats. In Eastbourne I had my dinners of cheese and bread sitting on the sides of old fishing vessels drawn up on to the beach. Just to feel their wooden gunwales, the curve of their bows, was enough. At Pevensey Bay I found a few forlorn dinghies hauled up in the dunes and dreamed of taking one out right there into the open sea, where the Royal Shoals Sovereign lighthouse loomed like some mysterious beast of the deep. At Hastings, I made at once for the *stade*, the ancient fishing quarter, where boats lay on the shingle under a forest of menacing, tattered black flags. Tall, tar-covered huts once used for drying nets stood guard at the back of the beach and the place had an electrifying, primitive, wild aura that made me reluctant to get back into the car.

Now, where the coast road to Dover began to cut inland across the base of the Dungeness peninsula, I veered south, intent on steering by the sea. The road snaked past low sand banks, scrub, lonely cottages and mile upon mile of chain-link fences behind which stretched army shooting ranges. Occasionally, soldiers in camouflage appeared on the verges. Nothing eased the ragged surface of undulating shingle, untidy grass, uninviting ponds, colossal pylons marching inland from the power station and handmade signs warning PRIVATE PROPERTY or NO ENTRY. There were few businesses: a shack selling fish, a breaker's yard where three chopping-block-headed men leered at my car and a peeling billboard that read: 'Bars and Carvery, Cabaret and Dancing, Pool Tables. Children's Room. Special Functions. Go-Kart Track. Jet Skis. Windsurfing. War Games. Clay Pigeon Shooting. Caravan Camping. Ski and Fishing Clubs.' Walland marsh gave way to Romney marsh, but I kept on for the point of the teat, where Denge marsh hit the Channel. Finally, where the gigantic box of the Dungeness nuclear power station broke the horizon, the shingle turned into sea.

I left the car and walked along the shore, sinking and scrambling in the loose stones, which, like the constant hum of the power station, intruded into every second of life at Dungeness. Merely to walk across shingle was difficult. Special pathways of planks had been laid from the road to the water's edge for the use of boatmen and fishermen, but these were few and far between. Putting up a building was even harder. Some houses rested on rafts, literally floating on the shifting ground.

Out in the Channel, large ships moved in orderly queues from east to west. As soon as one disappeared into the ash horizon, another took her place. Set apart from these iron tubs was a three-masted square rigger tacking eastwards against the wind. The conditions out there must have been rough, because the bow of this ship kept rising and falling violently. Her progress was slow and by the time she'd rounded Dungeness, the cast of cargo freighters had changed several times. The sailing ship looked so out of place that I wished I knew who was aboard and where they were going. The freighters moved as if on underwater rails, but this dreamy contraption of wood and canvas was having to battle and negotiate her way down the Channel tack by tack. Her progress, or rather lack of progress, seemed almost human. The freighters looked as if they were keeping appointments, but the sailing ship was on a voyage. I longed for *Aquila*. To many experienced sailors, dinghies were for racing, or thrill-seeking, rather like skiing. But for me, the greatest thrill was to cross from one place to another. *Aquila*, like that ship out there, was a maker of voyages. She was a miracle that took me over water, an infinitely movable bridge between any two banks I chose. Soon, after Adèle and I met up in Calais, we'd be back with *Aquila*, back afloat, and I couldn't wait.

The ferry from Dover was more motorway service station than ship. Even outside, where engine stench streamed in the salt wind over steel decks and lifeboats fattened on davits, the sea struggled to intrude. Seagulls hovered over the stern as if tied by string to the railings. But they laughed in chaotic chorus when the captain asked us over loudspeakers not to panic 'in the unlikely event of an emergency'. In an hour I'd be in France with Adèle. The Channel was that easy – at least, this Channel, the Channel seen from the deck of a floating service station. But there were many other Channels and not all of them so kind. I knew now that I could not let myself be fooled. Not after what I'd seen in Dover on the way to the ferry that morning.

What happened was that I'd timed my stay in the port so that I could witness the start of a cross-Channel swim. This was a feat of strength that had always fascinated me and I'd got up on the appointed morning in high spirits. Because the exact timing had been uncertain – 'around dawn', I was told – I'd had to leave my B&B well before sunrise, then walk out of Dover and up an empty dual carriageway to the top of Shakespeare Cliff. There, under the glow of orange lamps, I found steep stairs down to the beach from which all swims begin. Starlight reflected off the chalk cliff. The first train of the day clattered from Dover, spitting sparks like a dragon and disappearing angrily through a tunnel into the hill. Then darkness and silence. I paced the sand, expecting something to happen, but I was alone. After half an hour there was no sign of the sun, or the swimmers, and my enthusiasm began to seep away.

I'd once toyed with the idea of trying to swim across myself, but any lingering misconceptions about how difficult it was had been put right in discussion with the secretary of the Channel Swimming Association, Duncan Taylor. Even though my plan was now to sail, what I'd learned still applied: that there is no such thing as an easy crossing of those twenty-two miles. Even a fast swimmer will take about ten hours, and some can take twenty or even longer. Swimmers can actually become seasick, something I hadn't been aware was possible.

Sometimes a sick or exhausted swimmer can barely get on to the support boat. Some become so tired they go into trances, plagued by hallucinations and spectres, like the witches seen by the first Channel swimmer, Captain Matthew Webb. This is still a feat of strength reserved for the dedicated few. Many people had succeeded since Webb's conquest on 24–25 August 1875 – 500 by the end of the twentieth century. But the number of those who'd tried and failed told the story best: 4,000.

Webb, dubbed the 'man-fish', was a swimming machine who as a child had beaten a Newfoundland dog in a contest to see who could paddle for longest and in his mid-twenties had been decorated for trying to rescue a sailor during an Atlantic gale. So although he made his crossing without special diets or even carefully calculating the cross-tides, he might be said to have been born for the task. A study by his doctor, Henry Smith, showed that at the age of twenty-seven he weighed fourteen stone and eight pounds and measured five feet eight. His physique:

gave a good relative proportion, showing his large chest capacity is constant from top to bottom . . . His chest is deep without the slightest tendency to pigeon-breast. His legs are straight and well on a substantial pelvis. Webb would, I should say, never be a very fast swimmer from the size and weight of his loins and legs, but this weight means in the long run a reserve force. The Sartorius muscles which nip the legs together and tend greatly to produce that long propelling action are firm and large.

The story of his success – the red silk swimming suit, the rousing chorus of 'Rule Britannia' from a passing passenger boat, the struggle to complete the last section after the tide turned near France, the triumphant arrival after twenty-one and three-quarter hours in the water – instantly entered English mythology. It was as if this conquest of the Channel affirmed Britain's superiority over every sea and although dozens of attempts were made, no one matched Webb's feat for another thirty-six years. 'Land, ho! Land, ho! And through the mist, all England with him sees it! He'll win it yet, that glorious goal! His English pluck decrees it!' cheered the doggerel of the day. Where Webb embodied English beef, his great rival, the American Captain Paul Boyton, was the symbol of Yankee ingenuity. Wrapped in an extraordinary waterproof and inflatable suit, Boyton had managed to float and paddle across the Channel, even smoking a cigar to prove how comfortable he was. When the wind was behind him he attached a tiny brass mast to a socket in the sole of his left boot and raised a two-square-foot canvas sail. This adventure set in train generations of madcap Channel crossings, by floating bicycle, floating cross-country skis, floating cars, rafts, even straw, but for Webb, the clean-cut hero, only swimming counted. 'I thought of Boyton in his indiarubber dress, and I felt what a proud thing it would be for me, an Englishman, to accomplish the same task with nought save my muscles to help me.'

Yet that reliance on muscles killed Webb in the end. Rather than return to the Channel, the way many of today's champions do, Webb had embarked on a lucrative but gruelling career of endurance swims for public entertainment, where, stroke by stroke, he wore down his own strength. In need of money and another stunt, he died in 1883 trying to swim through the rapids under Niagara Falls. When they found his body, all gashed, crushed and swollen, eight miles down river, his famous red suit was in shreds.

Scanning the restless, dark water as I waited on the beach, I had no difficulty imagining how inhospitable the Channel must be and felt my heart warm to Webb and Boyton for their daring and *élan*. I'd never swum and never would swim anything like the Dover Straits, but I'd shared, and still did share, these swimmers' fascination for crossing gaps.

My longest swim had been a decade earlier in Turkey, crossing the Hellespont. Two university friends and I had arrived with a plan to hide our clothes in the bushes, swim from Asia to Europe, and take the ferry back to find our clothes. We'd read Byron, drunk a lot of Turkish wine and decided that a few nights spent sleeping in the olive groves were qualification enough for an escapade in which the actual swimming seemed the least important part. This grand idea looked different out of the olive groves and down by the water's edge, for the Hellespont straits, where the Sea of Marmara meets the Aegean, were rather busy. Ferries, cargo ships and warships moved in procession and, supposedly, Russian submarines were also slipping through on clandestine voyages out of the Black Sea. We needed not only an escort but, we soon discovered, authorization to swim at all, and so ensued two days in the labyrinth of officialdom – the anterooms, lunch hours, blank faces, special fees – before the local governor gave his seal of approval. Instead of the simple jaunt we'd planned, our swim finally took place in the company of two escort boats and numerous hangers-on, all of them taking some cut. Nevertheless, we did cross, and although I'd always found swimming long distances monotonous, the crossing was a revelation. Now I knew what it meant to link two parts of the globe without touching ground. I felt as if I'd learned to fly.

It was in search of that sensation that I'd gone, not long after, to Sicily to attempt to swim the Straits of Messina. I was with one of my Hellespont companions and both the distance – only a couple of miles, although made difficult by strong currents and large ships – and the bureaucratic complications were similar to those encountered on the first swim. But this time we had less luck. Although we were able to secure permission and the obligatory escort to guide us through the shipping lanes, a misunderstanding or two caused us to miss our rendezvous on the day and to my despair the swim was cancelled. Feeling caged, desperate to touch that hazy far shore and convinced that wanting to cross would be enough to make us succeed, I'd suggested we take the risk of just getting in and swimming anyway, even without the escort. So it was, smothered in Vaseline and goggled up, that we entered the water at the narrowest point and struck out for the toe of Italy. There followed a ludicrous attempt to defeat the currents in the face of fading light, cramp in my friend's calves and the approach of a fast cargo ship named, as we saw when she steamed past in mid-channel, *La Serenissima*. Defeat was inevitable, but I'd cursed it all the same and now, a decade later, standing under Shakespeare Cliff and knowing that I'd never be able to swim across the Channel, I felt humbled by my physical weakness. Yet, who knew? Maybe in that truncated Italian crossing were the seeds, quite unnoticed at the time, of my current journey to France.

Just as I was wondering whether I'd come on the wrong day altogether, the sun edged reluctantly from the Dover Straits and I saw that my wait was over. Several fishing boats appeared out of Dover harbour and half a dozen spectators who'd had a better idea of the time to arrive than I descended the stairs to the shore. The cliffs no longer looked as white in daylight and the beach I'd been on for an hour was unrecognizable – mean and dirty, where before it had been mysterious and virginal. Now the escort boats motored close in and the swimmers jumped out to come to the beach, where they had to touch land before going back in for the swim.

The first ashore was a minuscule woman, very brown and wiry, wearing a red cap and a green bathing suit. 'Good luck,' I said to her. 'Thank you,' she replied, with a smile so winning that I felt I knew her. She waved to her escort boat, ran back into the water and began to swim overarm to France. Someone behind me shouted, 'Adios.' Quickly following was a man called Xavier with thighs the shape of frog's legs and arms like paddles. He whooped and leapt in the air before diving in. After him came an American woman built in much the same way. By the time they disappeared into the sea, the sun was full and the beach and cliffs looked scruffier than ever.

It was the next day I took the ferry to Calais. On my way to the docks, I saw this headline on the front page of *The Times*: 'Woman dies during attempt to swim the Channel.' Page three had a blurry colour photograph of my little friend with the red cap and green suit. Her name, I read, was Fausta Marin Moreno. She was forty-one and came from Mexico.

Beyond the north-west pocket of France, there was no love among the French for Calais, as if it were barely part of the same country. Adèle considered the town English, which for 200 years of the Middle Ages it had been. Even the rest of the almost derisively named *la Manche*, or the Sleeve, came in for turned-up noses. The good bits, Brittany and lower Normandy, were considered to be all but on the Atlantic, while the rest, well, they were too close to Calais. Yet for me, arriving in Calais with that first glimpse of the lighthouse, the beach huts and men fishing from the end of the breakwater was a liberation. England was forgotten, the Channel was forgotten; only the getting there mattered. The thought that one day I would make such a landfall alone in my own boat was almost too rich to digest.

Going to the train station to meet Adèle, I laughed to myself, enjoying the *frissons* of expectation that seemed to come just from making the crossing, from going south. Even when we'd moved on, become wiser, more travelled, harder to surprise, those old clichés of the French kiss, the French letter, the Marquis de Sade and the Moulin Rouge welled up in mid-Channel, all the more enduring because the Channel still made them seem exotic. There was that song I loved by Serge Gainsbourg and his English rose, Jane Birkin, all about '*le ferry boat*', about crossing the Channel and looking from their bunk through the porthole, full of love and dreams. A real cross-Channel adventure. Birkin had just left an emotionally sterile marriage and the chic of Chelsea and Park Lane for the debaucheries of life with Gainsbourg. '*Soixante-neuf, année érotique*,' they sang on the ferry. At least there was one Frenchman who'd loved *la Manche*. As a beginner, he'd earned his keep playing the piano for well-heeled English tourists in Le Touquet–Paris Plage, the Channel resort to which the English, unable to gamble at home, would fly for weekends of roulette and cards. Bejewelled wives used to lust after Gainsbourg and he, in turn, lusted after them. It was also on these shores that he took Birkin for their first trip alone. '*Ma petite British se fut gelé le cul,'* ('My little British girl froze her ass off') Gainsbourg said in his typically mocking way. I remembered advertisements for ferry tickets in one of the London tabloids that featured a smiling blonde dressed only in a beret, neckerchief, stockings, garter belt and a long string of onions. The deal, she promised, was *'magnifique!'* Now, on my way to fetch Adèle, I reckoned that there was something to those cross-Channel myths after all.

We checked into the Hôtel Meurice, a place full of surprises. The outside was grim concrete, but the restaurant inside looked like an opera house and gilt lay thick on every surface. In the foyer, a glass showcase hung on the wall. It contained a few surprises of its own: a pair of blue and gold knickers and a bra, white knickers, an assortment of lacework. In the dull avenues and side streets of the town, the sight was often repeated. Shops filled their windows with lace and every form of undergarment in blacks and blues, in whites and reds and greens. The number of such places seemed disproportionate. Even at the Holiday Inn there was an ice cream on the menu called 'Calais Lacemakers' desert'. Unlikely as it seemed, Calais was a world centre for lingerie.

In the Rue Richelieu we found a museum where a mannequin wore the high-collared black taffeta dress of a Madame Fontanelle in 1893, just one glass case from a sister mannequin in a *'robe de Garden Party'*, Greek goddess style, and another in the *'robe d'été de forme Princesse'*. Overhead, a garter belt and an alarmingly pointy matching *soutien-gorge* hung from the wall. Other cases contained samples of lacework: baroque motifs, bobbin lace, *point de France* – every combination dancing and weaving in silk, in cotton and in wool, trapped by hidden metal wires, sometimes opaque, sometimes diaphanous, or perhaps an exquisite marriage of the two. Each time, the patterns ended in wavelets or rows of silky teeth – the *dents* of *dentelle* – and each design sample was copyrighted, tied up in a box and sealed with red wax, like the code to a secret. ' . . . *la Dentelle de Calais qui est unanimement appréciée par les femmes du Monde entier pour sa délicatesse, son charme et sa séduction,*' murmured the museum blurb.

The sight of a large black and white picture taken in one of Calais's lingerie workshops shook me from my dreams. In the photo, looms stretched across the factory floor (and it was a factory, not some artisan's atelier), where men in blue overalls fine-tuned the cogs and levers and pistons of giant machines. Somehow from this tangle of machinery *délicatesse, charme* and *séduction* were squeezed. The men in overalls were *tullistes*, the loom technicians, a job reserved for men, while women did the delicate tasks. Hundreds of metres of cloth were dyed green, red, pink, cream or purple in steaming vats, then worked over by the women and examined by technicians who wore white coats and magnified the details of embroidery on television screens until they looked like strands of DNA. Nowhere in all that array of technology could the untrained eye spot even the seeds of a corset or a lace tablecloth. Beauty and the beast, except that in this version the beast was the father. In nothing, except perhaps the strange journey of a diamond from an African or Siberian pit to a woman's finger, could there be a more incongruous life cycle than that of *dentelle*.

For several hundred years before the Industrial Revolution, lace had been an expensive handmade material that for a long time was found only on the wrists and necks of rich or very holy European men. Even when women began wearing lace in the eighteenth century, it remained too costly for most. It was the English with their brilliant new weaving machines who changed that, but for trade reasons it was French territory where the business could flourish. The English looked for the nearest place to which they could smuggle their technology and shortly Calais, invaded by thousands of Nottingham textile workers, became the lingerie capital of the world. Much of the town was obliterated during the Second World War, but the lace survived. In Calais, the lingerie industry was the secret unexpected little garment under the shapeless, rough dress of a modern town. 'Adèle,' I said, 'we must buy you a souvenir.'

That afternoon, we crossed back over the Channel together. All the way I stared out of the portholes at the rolling sea. I tried to imagine myself out there in *Aquila* one day. I couldn't. The weather was fine and there was not a strong wind, yet all the same the sea looked lumpy and violent. Not just violent, but careless, like some simple giant – the same giant that killed poor Fausta and probably never even noticed. I looked on the sea with reproach, but understood at once there was no point, for the waves that so worried me kept coming, relentless and amoral. Inwardly I pleaded for some sign that the sea would treat me well, but there was no response. The sea might be kind or cruel, but always in its own time. It was the sailor and boat that had to adapt. Thinking of what lay ahead, I was filled at once with excitement and dread.

3

B ack on *Aquila*, our trajectories grew ever longer. We lost our fear of fresh winds and could sail, mainsail reefed, through choppy water that just two months before would have confined us to harbour. Up in the rivers and creeks, we learned to lift the centreboard and rudder, gliding in over less than thirty centimetres of water to reach the most sheltered spot for the night. The whole Solent, almost as far as Southampton, became our hunting ground. Lymington, Newtown, Beaulieu – these once far-off places felt like new friends. One day we got to Cowes, the furthest we'd ever been, although the confusing experience of plunging into such thick harbour traffic – the yachts, dredging barges, fishing boats, high-speed ferries, coasters – made us wonder whether we'd in fact gone a little too far.

But, for all these advances, we never left the Solent, and impossible as it would have once seemed, the Solent was gradually starting to feel cramped. Somewhere out there, invisible on the other side of the Isle of Wight, lay the big sea, the empty horizon and great thoroughfare of the English Channel. That was where I had to get. Not that I thought I was ready to cross, not even close, but I ached at least to open the door to the wider world. Just to get as far as Barton-on-Sea, the dreary little resort a few miles down coast where Adèle and I had once swum, would at least give me a taste of the sensation I craved.

There were two options for leaving the Solent, both prob-
lematic. One was to go east, all the way past Southampton
and around the eastern corner of the Isle of Wight. However,
that was unworkably far at our level. The other, the obvious
choice, was to exit through the western end of the Solent,
where Hurst Castle and its shingle spit reach out to the wooded
cliffs of Wight. This was all of ten minutes' sail from Keyhaven
and would take me immediately into waters that ran uninterrupted all the way to France. Easy – as long as we could get
through the Trap.

Every trip Adèle and I made began by avoiding the Trap,
leaving it to stern as we headed east. Yachts, fishing boats and
large ships made regular traffic out, but we'd never seen a
dinghy go that way and I'd begun to lose confidence that we
ever would. The sea there had a frightening life force of its
own. Even when everywhere else was placid, the surface
in the Trap could rise in tangled, triangular waves, eddies
intertwining into Celtic swirls. On rough days, the whole area
foamed white as if the water was boiling. The fact that there
were also moments when the surface of the Trap was utterly
smooth served only to deepen the mystery. The name alone
conjured images of *Aquila* being sucked into a whirlpool or
swept on to rocks and I began to fear those waters in the way
that seamen once feared giant squid and the ghosts of dead
sailors. No doubt this was how myths began.

When I studied the chart, more rational explanations
emerged. A symbol of ripples showed where tidal currents in
the Trap would bottleneck over a seabed plunging to fifty-nine
metres then shooting up to less than ten metres in the space
of a boat's length. A little further out a green patch marked
where a bank called the Shingles broke the surface, threatening

any boat and creating even more dangerous turbulence. A special annotation on the chart read: 'Depths over Shingles frequently change, and parts of it are occasionally uncovered ... The sea breaks violently over the bank in the least swell.' All this was something akin to a mixture of rapids and deep pools in an enormously powerful river. But knowing that was of no comfort.

Corked up in the Solent, I became increasingly worried. If I couldn't get through the Trap, how would I ever handle what lay beyond? The Trap frightened me, frightened me not only for its currents and turbulence, but because it represented for me the unknown. I still had no idea of what lay beyond. Maybe that open sea I was desperate to get into would not be so enticing after all. Maybe the Trap would be only the start of my problems ... When I tried to question the old salts around the boatyard, they'd suck their breath and answer vaguely with comments like, 'Just make sure you get the conditions right,' to which I'd exclaim, 'Of course!' and shuffle away, more baffled than ever.

It was as if I'd found a window on the old sea – not the tame canal of the ferries and cargo traffic, but a wild place. This was the sea that for Julius Caesar, coming from France in 55 BC, had marked the edge of the known world. 'No one, except for traders, went there as a matter of course, and not even they knew anything beyond the coastline,' Caesar said. When the mad emperor Caligula tried to emulate Caesar's invasion of Britain in AD 40, his troops simply refused to embark. Caligula punished them by ordering the men to gather shells on the beach. Even the Roman army that three years later went on to complete the occupation of Britain hesitated. The troops, wrote the later historian Cassius Dio, 'complained that they were about to campaign beyond the limit of civilization'. I was at the edge of the sea that had spooked the legionnaires. Only now it was my turn to cross.

In the end, the Trap, not I, chose the manner of our meeting.

I woke alone, anchored in the bay of Hurst Castle under heavy rain. I'd come alone on purpose, for somehow this question of the Trap was personal, something I wanted to sort out by myself. Although I'd made some progress sailing single-handed, I'd not spent a night alone on *Aquila* until then and it felt strange not to be able to talk with Adèle under the canvas tent. Adding to my loneliness, it was midweek, so the bay lay empty, barring a couple of moored yachts and the occasional fisherman chugging through. Rain thumped at *Aquila*, a frontal assault combined with devious incursions into every weak point of the tent. Wind moaned and stuttered in the rigging. A small ferry taking tourists to the castle chugged past. The skipper and his mate stared down in surprise and waved. Poking a hand from the back of the tent, I returned the wave, but my mind was on other things.

Today I was determined to investigate the Trap. I say investigate, because my plan was to probe at the edges, get used to the rough water and only later, when I felt confident, decide whether or not to launch myself through the gap and out of the Solent. I climbed into my oilskins and boots, put away all the gear into the lockers or waterproof bags, readied the sails and rudder, and finally stripped off the tent. My movements were deliberate, ritualistic. The poor visibility in the rain and the echo chamber of my oilskin hood made me claustrophobic. I felt as if I was being watched and realized I was talking to myself. At least that proved I was alone. Or did it? 'Come on, *Aquila*,' I said, 'we're off to take a look at that damned Trap.'

Crouched on the bow, I hauled in the anchor line of twenty-five metres. This was a manoeuvre that I'd done only a few times alone, certainly not in such windy conditions. Reaching the end of the line, I gave a sharp pull. Up popped the anchor. Now the difficult part. As soon as the anchor was up, the boat began moving, and instead of being where I needed to be, in the stern with the rudder and sails under control, I was still perched up front with a coil of rope, a chain and a muddy anchor in my arms. In calm conditions, I might have had no problem making the switch, but in this wind *Aquila* was already on her way, at speed, on course for the beach. By giving up any hope of a dignified move to the stern, I was able to toss aside the anchor and line and scramble to the tiller just in time to prevent *Aquila* running aground.

Only just. There was no time to think what would happen next – only to steer as violently in the other direction as possible. *Aquila* spun on her axis like a top. The wind snatched at the mainsail, the boom tore across and even then all would have been well had I been able to duck and spring up on the other side to balance. Instead the boom met my skull. Stars long since disappeared behind the night's clouds burst back, I almost dropped the tiller and *Aquila* rotated wildly once more. Only by managing to shut out the pain for a crucial few seconds did I escape another uncontrolled turn. But now we were sailing off and the rattling of rigging and the groaning wind fell silent, replaced by the measured ripple of water against hull. As quickly as things had gone wrong, calm had returned. That always seemed to be the way on the sea. We left the bay and entered the Solent. Under my wet hair, a cartoonish bump. The Trap was waiting.

In preparation, I had established this much: the only way for a small boat to pass through the Trap was with the help of the prevailing tide – in other words, going out when the tide ebbed and returning when the tide rose. I understood very little of the tides, but as far as I could gather, my timing this morning was perfect. The tide was now on the way out and would soon switch, meaning that if I did decide to go through, I would be able to return whenever I wanted during the following few hours. *If* I decided to go through.

In no time I'd reached the end of the shingle spit and the outer walls of Hurst Castle. Before me foamed the unsettling sight of the Trap. Waves didn't come in tidy rows, the way they seemed to elsewhere, but in chaotic mêlées where one wave might appear from nowhere, another went in a different direction to the rest and others collided before rushing off in a new direction altogether. Doubtful that today was the day for negotiating this beast, I made two half-hearted stabs into the fringes, hitting some of the rough before turning back into the smoother water of the Solent. On the third trial run, just when I thought it was probably time to get out, the Trap took over. Straying a few metres too far, I'd entered a place where the current would no longer let me return. Even with the wind behind me I could not move forward a bit: the point of no return. Unable to escape, certainly unable to stay motionless in the middle of these waves, there was nothing to do but point *Aquila* right out of the Trap, sit well on the sides and steer for the open sea. Already water coming in over the sides was filling the floor.

The effect of being carried by a strong current is that the

boat travels much faster than appears possible, like running down a conveyor belt. Within seconds we entered the heart of the Trap, the place on the chart marked with those neat little waves. The real waves twisted and jumped, requiring me to concentrate on every metre I steered. Naturally, the best way to tackle a wave was head on, so that *Aquila*'s bows could rise up or, at the worst, punch through. Sometimes, though, that meant *Aquila* coming back down with a crash on to the following wave. Alternatively the next wave might not come from the same direction at all, but from the side, a far more dangerous proposition. So focused was I on my partner in this watery tango that I didn't notice at all, not until it was almost too late, that we'd been swept right out of the Trap and almost on to the dreaded Shingles bank beyond.

My first warning was a huge yellow and black buoy rearing up a few metres off *Aquila*'s bow. Buoys are such a comforting sight from a distance and this one had indeed seemed a long way off a few minutes before. Close to, it was a dangerous customer, a towering cone of beaten-up iron. Currents pushed the buoy at a steep angle, water welling up on the east side and pouring around the edges into a vortex of white foam on the west. I had time to shout and jerk the tiller. I was clear, but only just. To be sunk against a buoy – that would be rum. Less than a minute later, the buoy was already well behind. And the Shingles, announced by the strange sight of waves breaking in the middle of the sea, were right ahead. Another sharp pull on the tiller, heart pounding, and I was safe.

In negotiating this madhouse, I'd all but failed to realize that I'd cleared the Trap. For the first time in my life, grey, grim Hurst Castle, even uglier on this side, was behind me. To the west the long bleak beach of Hampshire extended as far as I could see, to the south, off the Isle of Wight, were the fantastically shaped Needles rocks and beyond was nothing but water until the Cherbourg peninsula, more than seventy miles away. This was the open Channel. I turned and darted back into the Solent as soon as the tide changed. By the time I got to Keyhaven, several centimetres of water sloshed around *Aquila*'s floorboards. My right hand, I was amazed to see, was bound so tight around the mainsail control that it hurt to open. But I rejoiced; the curse was broken.

That day marked a coming of age, not only for me but for *Aquila*. Looking now at my boat, all gleaming woodwork, black floorboards and broad, smooth sides, I felt deep stirrings of trust. Already that summer I'd learned the impulse to protect her at all costs. No more reckless running up on to shingle beaches, no careless scraping of varnish or letting the boom bang on the deck. But now I understood that as long as I protected her she'd also look after me.

The time had come for certain technical adjustments. The way she was, *Aquila* was still a dinghy for sheltered waters, an extremely solid vessel for sorties of a few hours at a time, but not sufficiently autonomous for sailing the open sea. In talking with Jim and other Wayfarer owners who congregated at the boatyard, I found out there were numerous changes to make. Chiefly, I needed to improve the system for reefing, or reducing the size of the sails. Currently I could cut down the mainsail only through a laborious process that required going on to a beach or dropping the anchor. What I needed was an ingenious system of lines and small pulleys that would allow me while at sea and unaided to change the size of the mainsail in an instant. For the foresail, there was an equally miraculous method called roller furling. This consisted of two swivels, one at the bottom of the sail, the other at the top. When a line was pulled, the swivels would turn and the sail would roll up around itself. Another tug on the line and the sail would unfurl, ready for use again.

Making these improvements meant taking on a rigger. At a place near Keyhaven I was introduced to Frank. Everyone kept telling me that Frank, a short, stocky fellow with a cigarette behind one ear, was a treasure, and Frank was unlikely to argue about that. 'The best rigger in the Solent,' a passer-by said as we stood around *Aquila*. 'You might as well say the best rigger in the whole south, if you're going to say things like that,' Frank mumbled. Maybe I should have been warned. When we happened across a £5 note lying on the ground, I said, 'Now there's a piece of luck.' He answered, 'Only £5. There's not much you can do with £5 these days, is there?' but still put it in his pocket. The work – mostly riveting a handful of small cleats and pulleys in strategic places for the reefing lines – probably should have taken a couple of hours, but Frank was used to working on large yachts and to my amazement said he had no idea how or where the various attachments should go on the humble dinghy. Neither, of course, did I. So the great man and I spent long, almost comical periods wandering around an adjacent dinghy park peering into other people's Wayfarers for clues. Finally I drove into Lymington and found someone who, I was told, knew everything about Wayfarers. He drew me a little diagram which I gave to Frank. When I finally had *Aquila* and the trailer hitched back up to the car ready to return to Keyhaven, it was dusk.

The experience was my first with the boat industry. When I'd read Jack London's self-mocking description of the building of his yacht *Snark*, I'd thought he was making gross exaggerations. Now, after my own small-scale experience, I had an idea of what he'd meant. In any work on any boat, the pocket not only burns but spontaneously combusts. Buy a small shackle – the smallest, barely useful as a keyring, still costs about £2 – and a train of other purchases appears on the line: a different rope, a stronger cleat, a nut and bolt to replace that suspect screw, and by now, no doubt, a little varnish to cover the bare patch that caught your eye as you did all this other work . . . On the furling swivel for the foresail, the cheapest model at the chandler's came in at about £30 and didn't work. Back I went to the chandler's in Lymington and bought another version, identical except for an additional tiny strip of metal down the outside. It cost another £7. When *Aquila* was finally ready, I'd spent well over £200 in a day, 10 per cent of the original price of the boat. Other boat owners laughed when I expressed amazement. 'Put the word yacht or boat in front of anything you want and double the prices,' laughed a Wayfarer man as he showed me the gadgets arrayed on his boat.

There was something I wanted to do that would cost nothing and that was to change the name of *Aquila*. I didn't think it a bad name, not at all, but as *Aquila* and I grew closer I'd begun wanting to give her a name of my own, something that reflected our journey. The name I settled on was Gilliatt, the hero of Victor Hugo's *Les Travailleurs de la mer*, a novel set in and around Guernsey in the early nineteenth century. Gilliatt is 'a sailor of rare skill' who commands an old pilot sloop that he'd won in a competition and which, like *Aquila*, he then modified for sailing further and in rougher seas. But quite apart from his skill, I found myself liking Gilliatt because in the book so few people on Guernsey liked him. He is a 'kind of savage' who keeps himself to himself, is shy and tries to opt out of Guernsey's close-knit and claustrophobic society. He is unkempt, a dreamer. The superstitious and staid neighbours – nearly everyone around – do not forgive him for refusing to join in and they are so envious that they attribute his skills to sorcery.

Looking around in Keyhaven, I'd learned to recognize many different types of sailor: those with yachts designed mostly for drinking gin in the cockpit; power-boaters who liked carving huge wakes and watching onboard TVs; picnickers in ugly but friendly pocket yachts; handymen who never went to sea at all, but spent the whole time working in the boatyard; rich families, sometimes happy, often a little flustered, coming into harbour on large, shiny yachts that looked like more responsibility than fun; and then the real salts, sometimes men alone, sometimes couples, often on small boats, but always on boats that looked lived in and alive, boats that would travel. Gilliatt was one of these, a free man and, as Adèle had once urged me to become, a real sailor. I knew he would have felt quite at home in the Trap, for he 'appeared to possess a chart of the bottom of the sea; and indeed he was afraid of nothing for his knowledge was perfect'. OK, the name *Gilliatt* sounded strange, even ugly at first, but what name could be better for my Channel-crossing vessel?

It was as I'd begun thinking about the script I might use – block capitals, linked, italics or something round, stencilled or hand-painted – that I recalled a story about it being bad luck – or was it good luck? – to rename a boat. It was just as well to check. I thought that any boatman would know.

At the first opportunity, I questioned the owner of the dinghy parked next to *Aquila* in the Keyhaven boatyard. 'Well,

you're not meant to,' he said. 'It supposedly brings bad luck.'
I asked if there really was no way. 'I suppose you might be
able to perform some ceremony or something,' he answered,
but sounded unsure. So I phoned the Royal Yachting Association, the guardian of rules in sailing and a great stickler for
traditions. The woman to whom I got through was evidently
not prepared, but I liked her formal approach. 'Will you just
wait a minute? I'll see if I can get further information for you,'
she said. That was what I wanted: no guessing, just the official
word. Bad luck was not a thing I liked to tempt, not in sailing
and the sea. However, the woman returned with only another
fudge: 'If that's what you want to do, you should probably
just go ahead.' Surely that wasn't right, I said. 'It's up to you.'
No good at all.

I approached Charles at the boatyard. Charles was one of
the real sailors and also one of the kindest. He had a short,
plump yacht called *Countess*. He was always ready with advice
and in my early days had been one of the only persons I
dared ask questions. His replies were never condescending
and indeed he seemed to understand my quest. Although
Charles was a man happy sailing long distances in his yacht, I
was pleased to see that he kept a copy of that same book I had,
Sailing: A Beginner's Guide.

'Charles,' I said, 'I want to change the name *Aquila* to
Gilliatt. Is that OK?'

'You know what, I'm always fighting superstition. I don't
go in for any of that,' he replied. 'But there is one thing I'll
never do and that's change the name. Besides, I wouldn't want
to. I can leave the pub saying that I have to go back and see
the countess.'

I gave up. Well, not exactly. From then on, *Aquila* still

appeared on the bows of my boat – officially, nothing had changed – but an occasional nickname was coined: *Aquila-Gilliatt.*

Then, in honour of my hero, I made for Southampton and boarded the fast ferry to Guernsey. Gilliatt was a fictional character, yes. But he must have been based on real people and maybe today in the Channel Islands the same types lived on. If I could find them, then perhaps I could learn their secrets, returning to *Aquila* with the goal of one day sailing as well as Gilliatt himself.

Victor Hugo, who wrote *Les Travailleurs de la mer* during his long exile from France in the Channel Islands, said that 'the population of Guernsey is composed of two sorts of workers – workers on the land, and workers on the sea'. The first person I went to see on arrival in St Peter Port, Dougal Lane, was firmly one of the latter. He was no Gilliatt – too established for that – but he could easily have been Lethierry, the enterprising ex-sailor in *Les Travailleurs de la mer*, who shocks the backward islanders by setting up the first steamship ferry service between Guernsey and France.

Dougal Lane, like his house on the north coast of the island, had a look of modest but well-earned prosperity: tough, but substantial. He had a broken nose in a healthy, ruddy face. His cellar was full of items collected from diving expeditions on shipwrecks and fishing gear lay heaped at the back, but the dining room in which we sat to talk was ornate. Above us hung one painting of a brown and white spaniel and one of a sea captain with a grey beard and a pipe. The house was called Mon Désir.

Forty-six years old, Lane had fished for a quarter of a century and during that period a great deal had changed. Fishing methods catapulted forward, boats increased in power and navigation equipment lessened the mysteries of the sea, both above and below the surface. But with all these wondrous improvements, the fish population had begun to shrink and so, despite – or even because of – the technological advances, fishing remained a bitterly difficult way to make a living. Even greater changes took place on land, for it was during these years on Guernsey and the other Channel Islands that Hugo's neat division of the workforce finally became obsolete. There were still those working on the soil and the sea, but their ranks were nothing compared to those in tourism and the offshore finance industry. The islands' hazy constitutional status – British, but not part of the UK, half in the EU, half out, of Norman heritage rather than French – was fertile ground for the ambiguities of a tax paradise. And for all the backwardness described by Hugo in their reaction to Lethierry's attempts to set up a modern ferry service, the people of the Channel Islands had proved brilliantly adaptable when it came to banking and investment. Fixing brass plaques outside the offices of their handsome capitals St Peter Port and St Helier, the islanders had taken to tending other people's money with all the energy they once put into knitting wool, planting early vegetables or scraping the seabed for fish.

Dougal Lane was not won over. 'People used to know each other and it used to be so laid-back, whereas now the police over-regulate everything. They've sold out their quality of life for money. People here are rich, but it's all given over to bankers. My son, he's twenty and he's just got a trawler. But a starter home here costs 150 grand. Over in Brixham, you can get a mansion for that, so what should keep him here? For a fisherman who goes out to sea to work, what's the difference? With all the wealth being created here, we're not seen as important now. We're the lowest of the low.'

To make matters worse, Guernsey's fishermen were in a difficult dispute with their French rivals, essentially a matter of too few fish and too many claims to sovereignty over the same chunks of rock and reef, which meant that any agreements struck were often as tortuous as the disputes. In some places the French were allowed to fish, but only for one species, while on the French reef called Roches Douvres both French and Jersey boats were allowed to fish, but not those from Guernsey. Guernsey boats generally fished with pots and the French trawled, two fishing methods that were in themselves incompatible when operating in small areas.

Many Frenchmen believed that the big reefs of Minquiers and the Ecréhous were theirs, even though the international court in The Hague had ruled in 1953 that they were British, and incursions on to these desolate rocks had become something of a summer ritual. A few years back, a hotchpotch of fishermen, skinheads and royalists had landed on the Ecréhous long enough to raise the French Tricolour, celebrate Mass and disturb the colony of terns, before being dispersed by the true master, the rising tide. An even more peculiar raid had taken place the summer before my visit when associates of the celebrated French writer Jean Raspail went on to the Minquiers and replaced the Union Jack with the blue, white and green flag of Patagonia. The conquest, in the name of a French adventurer who in the nineteenth century had briefly set up as king in Patagonia, centred on the reef's flagpole and solitary loo. It lasted only a few hours, but was sure not to be the last word.

So far no shots had been fired, but the occasional interruption by sleek, grey naval boats, from whichever side, was enough to get people very excited. 'Two or three times we've had the French armed patrol boats in British waters guarding their fishing boats while they wreck our gear. So they do it with government backing,' Lane said. 'At that stage, I think we should shoot them. When they get armed boats and that, we should put a rocket through the bloody top of the patrol boat. Sink them.' Lane was really angry, although the only physical sign of this was a stare so intense that I had to keep looking away at the captain with the pipe or the spaniel. 'I don't mean sink the fishermen. Most of them are fine, struggling against the sea and the elements to make a living. But they don't have a right to sweep away our gear.'

All the same, Lane felt nothing short of awe for his French antagonists. 'Two or three years ago in Brest they burned down their parliament and shot a copper. The difference is that we can't do that in Britain. We'd get arrested,' he said. 'The French come over to us with a fleet of trawlers, five or eight men on each boat, and invade our port. They've done it three times. It's wonderful to see that solidarity. I wanted to sail into a French port, but my guys wouldn't support me at all. They're afraid of going into French ports because they might get their boats burned. They wouldn't even get off their arses to go to London.'

Herm, the mile-and-a-half-long speck in the sea east of Guernsey, relied completely on boats. There were no cars, no police and only a few dozen inhabitants. This was also where in *Les Travailleurs* Gilliatt won his old pilot sloop. The competition had been to sail the boat single-handed from Guernsey to Herm, pick up a cargo of stones and return. The vessel, although 'a good sea boat', was complicated to sail alone and in the rough conditions no one was able to complete the journey. 'The last man to try was one well known for having rowed across the terribly dangerous sea between Brecq-Hou and Sark. But, overcome with fatigue, he gave up, saying, "It cannot be done."' Gilliatt managed, though, winning the prize and deepening his evil reputation, for onshore word was that his success had been down to 'a branch of wild medlar concealed with him at the time'. As I boarded the small ferry boat for Herm, I had high hopes that this was a place where I might find the modern-day Gilliatt.

Adrian Heyworth was the ruler of Herm. Before, he'd been a Guernsey estate agent, but he'd married into the family which had been leasing Herm since 1949 and now that the founding father, Major Wood, was dead, had taken over. His children with Major Wood's daughter Pennie were the third generation on the island and the family's lease did not expire until 2049. Together, they quite literally ruled their own island.

'I am the co-chairman of the family business, Wood of Herm Island Ltd, along with Pennie,' he said. 'I am island manager, drain unblocker, cargo boat runner, puffin boat runner, relief power-house manager, special constable, sub-postmaster, church taker, and I also run the camp site.' In other words, a true islander, a Jack of all trades, dependent on the sea for supplies, but independent of everything else – just like Gilliatt. ('Not only was he a fisherman, he was a smith, a wheel-wright, a cabinet-maker, a boat-caulker, and something of an engineer, all of which trades he had taught himself in his leisure time. He made his own fishing gear; he could repair a wheel with the most skilful.')

However, the longer the ruler talked, the more I understood that Gilliatt would not have lasted on Herm. 'Malicious Gilliatt' would have been considered insufficiently cheerful and that would have spoilt the fabric of the island, carefully knitted by the ruler himself. This purpose-built community consisted of fifty people, thirty of whom stayed year round, running the island's gift shops, pubs and hotel. All were hand-picked in an exhaustive process of interviews. 'All our island families have been through that selection process,' the ruler said. 'We're lucky in that we choose who lives here. If we did have a neighbour from hell, we'd be able to get rid of him. The joy of living on Herm is you're not bound by petty restrictions, county councils, neighbours.'

That the rulers had put in place a *few* little rules went unremarked, for these didn't count. They were only to ensure that there was no need for any other rules. There was the perfect look of the place – that didn't come by chance. No flower picking, no radios on the beach, no straying off paths . . . 'That's why there are no public seats or benches,' the ruler explained. 'They encourage graffiti and litter.' Then there was the question of behaviour. 'We like the island to be quiet at eleven,' Pennie said. So no heavy drinking and no rows. In fact, one of the requirements to join Herm was a happy marriage. 'It's not something we can allow if they have a problem, or if their marriage is rocky,' Pennie said. 'It's something we're proud of. It's an ethos.'

In the mass of brochures I was given, Herm was described in otherworldly terms: 'Heaven on Earth', 'yachtsman's paradise' and 'Paradise is this close.' The funny thing is that in prehistory someone else had had a twist on the same idea: Herm was a Neolithic charnel house, a stepping stone to the afterlife, and in the bleak heathland at the northern tip the rulers' vision of blissful, perfectly organized life stumbled over rutted ground where rabbits scampered in the shallow graves.

Of all the islands, Sark is the one where life today must come closest to resembling that described by Victor Hugo. A sixteenth-century hierarchy still operates, with the island's hereditary leader, the seigneur, at the top, and there are no cars, police or income tax. But, as with the intrusion of Lethierry's fire-eating ship into the quiet life of Guernsey in *Les Travailleurs*, rude change was under way. An extraordinary tax loophole, dubbed the 'Sark Lark', had recently started to come under the scrutiny of inspectors from London, while the island's constitution was under attack from the multi-millionaire twin brothers David and Frederick Barclay, who'd bought themselves Brecqhou, the small island lying a couple of hundred metres to the west. Despite being separate, Brecqhou came under Sark jurisdiction, but the Barclays, having spent a great deal of money buying the rock, then building a castle, wanted certain matters – the archaic laws of inheritance in particular – to change. Believing this to be the thin end of a wedge, old-timers on Sark looked across at the black rock of Brecqhou, with its sprawling, turreted castle, like enemy territory.

The fact that Brecqhou had literally become a fortress made me want to go there. Visitors were not allowed and the Barclay twins rarely appeared on Sark proper, using a helicopter to get to Guernsey. There were fantastic and sometimes ludicrous stories in the press about Brecqhou: how the castle included defences against air attack, even a nuclear shelter, and how the hundreds of construction workers, many of them veterans of the Channel Tunnel, had been segregated so that none would ever know the shape of the project as a whole. I didn't know how much of this to believe, but I couldn't help wanting to get closer. Just to touch that forbidden shore was irresistible.

The gap between Sark and Brecqhou is called the Gouliot Passage. According to the rough tourist map I carried, the distance was no more than 200 metres at high tide and even less at low. But many bad things were said about the Gouliot. Hugo called it a 'terribly dangerous sea'. A man I met in Guernsey told me of almost losing the coffin he'd been delivering to Sark. 'We tried motoring through there against the current and got nowhere. We turned up the power until the boat was standing on end and water was coming in over the stern. The coffin got loose and began sliding around. Wreaths were flying about.' And the fisherman living at my B&B, a short, round, awesomely hardy fellow, told me that 'the currents are incredible. In our boat with a thirty-five-horsepower engine we can only just make it against the flow.' How could such a short distance be so difficult? For advice, I went to Philip Perrée.

Philip had been a fisherman before he turned some old cottages into the popular Sablonnerie hotel. He was one of the few people left who still spoke French, or the island version of French descended directly from the Norman of his ancestors in the Middle Ages. He was seventy-five. 'I didn't know a word of English till I went to school. I spoke French patois. Then I left school at eleven, apart from two hours in the afternoons with an old spinster who taught on the island. She wanted to teach us German, but I said, "No, no. If you teach me that I'm going home. My father would knock my head off if I spoke a word of it." So I asked to learn French – good

120

French; Parisian French.' His English came out in an accent more dry than French, but as mysterious, like a slightly clipped version of a Welsh accent. He pronounced his name *Pheeleep*.

One of Philip's most loyal customers at the hotel had been Professor James Lighthill, a mathematics genius and an accomplished swimmer. His papers included 'Studies on Magnetohydrodynamic Waves and Other Anisotropic Wave Motions', 'Jet Noise' and 'Hydrodynamics of Aquatic Animal Propulsion'. His real passion, though, was for bio-fluiddynamics, or the study of animal movement through air and water. He became well known at lectures for imitating the actions of fish or birds to illustrate his theories, but when swimming in the waters of the Channel Islands, where currents run like rivers and regularly change direction, his own body became the laboratory.

Lighthill devised a swimming style described by himself as 'a two-arm, two-leg backstroke, thrusting with the arms and legs alternately', and said to have been based on studies of the stickleback. In 1973 he became the first man to swim around all nine miles of Sark and over the next quarter-century he repeated the feat five times. Philip remembered: 'He told me one day, he said, "I've been practically around the world and every island I've been to I've swum around it." He was six foot three. Very tough.'

In the summer of 1998, when he was aged seventy-four, the professor got back into the water in the south of Little Sark for one last orbit. 'He came here on a Wednesday and he was so pleased to see me and I him,' Philip said. 'He said, "I'll swim around Sark on Friday." He'd worked it out that from Adonis Pool, where he'd start, the current would go north and he'd go round the north of the island that way. Then the current would come back south and the tide would bring him back. The sea was rough, but he liked to swim when it was rough, you know, he would glide down the waves. He always swam on his back.' After nine hours, the professor had come within shouting distance of triumph. Then he stopped swimming. Someone called the lifeboat. He was dead. 'I think what happened was that he took a bit longer to get around and then the tide changed before he could get in. What broke my heart was that he swam up to Port Gorey and he had only a short way before he'd finish. I was very, very fond of him.'

I asked about the Gouliot Passage. 'Oh, you can't get across there. Well, you might get across, but then you won't get back. There're strong tides in there. The only way would be to get over at slack tide. You'd get a few minutes when you could make it, but today that won't come till about 10 p.m., so you can forget it. The Gouliot's a dangerous place.'

Philip was old Sark, tall, thin, erect, with a shock of white hair, eyebrows that stuck outwards and mud on his trousers. I liked him tremendously. He had a good heart and I didn't want to worry him. So when he asked if I would try to swim to Brecqhou, I lied and said no, probably not.

The walk towards the Gouliot took me over the vertical thin neck of land connecting Little Sark to Sark proper, up along the spine of the island to Rue de Sermon, then west. At a church, I paused, unable to resist the gloomy magnetism of the place, beginning with the monument outside that listed seventeen men from the island killed in the Great War, three of them from the Carré family, four from the Guille family. Just inside, another list, this one showing which pews were reserved for which families (the entire front middle section for the seigneur). Further in, yet more names, this time on plaques commemorating those who'd died at sea. All the history of Sark was on these walls.

The plaques were of the same type that appeared in every church I'd visited on the Channel. Each one told a story in shorthand. The basic plot never differed and one knew the end at the start (it was always tragic), but the details – the names of people and boats, allusions to war or storms, references to grieving relatives – always seemed fresh. Most of the plaques dated to well before the First World War, when it was not uncommon for ships to leave one port and never arrive at the next. South America, India, South Africa – no place was too far away for a sailor to die in the days of empire. The crew were rarely remembered, but the officers, often men in their early twenties and thirties, tended to be the sons of respectable locals and so won the right to a cold stone or brass patch. Here in front of me was one that could have been on any church wall from the Scillies to Dover:

In Memory of
Eugène Grut Victor Cachemaille,
second son of the Rev. J. L. V. Cachemaille,
Vicar of Sark:
Born January 14th, 1840
and lost at sea in command of the 'Ariel'
which left London for Sydney in February, 1872.
and was heard of no more.

He was not, for God took him. Gen V.24

Fewer in number, but all the more shocking, were those, usually not more than one or two per church, that referred to cargo men and fishermen lost in home waters well into modern times. The Sark church had one from the 1960s – Carrés again, although sailors, not soldiers this time.

Cptn John William Carré, M.N.
aged 41 years
only son of pilot John Philip Carré and his wife
Gladys Maud née Falle
who perished with all hands in the M.V. St. Ernest
on the 19th January 1962 in the English Channel

'Greater love hath no man than this, that a man
lay down his life for his friends.'
St John 15.13

I sat back against the icy smooth wood of a pew to rest, then got up again to resume my path to the Gouliot. One last inscription caught my eye:

A la Mémoire de
John William Falle
âgé de 37 ans.
et de son fils William Slowley Falle,
âgé de 17 ans.
Fils et petit fils de William Falle, Ecr. De Beau Regard,
    Sercq.
qui furent noyés le 20ème jour d'avril 1903,
durant la traversée de Guernesey à Sercq.

What hunger in the belly of the sea, I thought, but also
what insatiable hunger in man to keep on that sea.

The Gouliot proved impossible to reach by foot. The headland
jutting out from Sark was a maze of gullies, ledges and boulders. Seagulls shrieked as I invaded their secret guano- and
bone-lined lairs. Once or twice a gull erupted so close to my
head that I almost lost my footing. I was struck by the sensation
that instead of me searching for Gilliatt, Gilliatt, who was
'constantly climbing the rugged cliffs', had found me. Eventually I found a way down to the water, but far around the
headland, doubling the distance I'd have to swim. All around
rose steep hills and cliffs, not a soul or a dwelling to be seen,
and it was with a sense of awe that I dived into the dark water.
Using breaststroke, I threaded through submerged boulders
and past a huge, long cave. From time to time, I grabbed
chunks of seaweed hanging thick as hair from the cliffs, to
pause for a rest, and, in this way, skipping along from minor
bluff to bluff, I made my way to the Gouliot.
    The moment I'd turned into the Gouliot the current
became a good deal stronger and I had to use my feet and
hands to grip the side of Sark so as not to be swept away.
There, high and black on the other side, rose the east face of
Brecqhou. For a minute I clung on, trying to decide what to
do. The current pulled to the north, but the waves racing
through the passage seemed to travel south. I began to feel
cold. The silence, broken only by the clap of waves running

into caves, weighed heavily and a voice kept telling me to turn back. Soon it would be late. But having come so far, another voice urged me on. The castle on Brecqhou was hidden on the other side of the island, but I could see what appeared to be a small boat landing stage and a tall pole with something on top, maybe a camera. That seemed to fit in with the tales I'd heard and I wondered whether I'd be spotted. I knew that I hadn't the strength to hang around. The water was pulling at my legs and my breath was coming out in steam. To cross or not? I filled my lungs, placed my feet against the last rock of Sark, coiled my legs and sprang.

The full flow of the Gouliot was worse than I could have imagined. I felt as if I'd been picked up and thrown. Two or three strokes towards Brecqhou and already I'd gone ten metres sideways. Get back, get back now, I thought in those seconds. Your only chance is to turn and get back. I did for an instant think of trying to press forward, but only an instant. Any more hesitation and I'd wind up neither on Brecqhou nor on Sark but somewhere far out to sea. I twisted into reverse, struck out maniacally, lungs inflated to bursting, legs and arms slashing. I had only twenty or so metres to retreat, but they were long metres, and when I did reach the seaweed-covered rock of Sark, I held on like a man at the side of a lifeboat. Actually, I felt surprised I'd made it and I knew that had I tried to keep going to Brecqhou I'd never have arrived, racing along like flotsam on the ocean stream, deep into the cold night and an open grave on the rocks. In careful movements, leaving nothing to chance, I swam back around the headland to the place I'd left my clothes. I was shivering.

By the time I climbed back up the boulders and walked to

my B&B on the other side of the island, it was dark. On television in my room a giant squid was attacking a steamship. I'd missed most of the film so I couldn't tell why the squid was so angry, but its tentacles made short work of the vessel, piercing decks, cabins and hull like paper. Finally the ship sank, the sea closed over and the heroes who'd survived made off in a dinghy. Surely, I thought, they were going to be mincemeat, vulnerable as they were in that tiny boat. But the squid had been satisfied and left them in peace. Taking my whisky flask, I proposed two toasts: one to the squid and another to the Barclay brothers and their impenetrable fortress of Brecqhou.

Tomorrow I would go to Jersey, my last stop. The idea of taking another ferry – two, in fact, because I had to get the small boat from Sark to Guernsey, then the huge catamaran to Jersey – excited me. For all their brutal ugliness, ferries still made me feel something of the magic of being afloat and travelling by water. The ferries were as direct as a plane, but a hundred times more adventurous. Even if the ship was so high-tech that she barely looked like a ship, ancient rituals still had to be observed. Passengers still had to gather at the water's edge, matelots still had to winch in the mooring lines and the captain still had to wait for the tide and steer through the harbour walls into the chaos of the sea.

This was the basic sensation of voyaging, of pushing the boat out from one place to another, then another, that I'd come to love in sailing with Adèle. There'd been a simplicity and innocence about those summer days that I knew would soon slip away, replaced by something equally vivid, but never the same. Going through the Trap had changed things. If it was that rough out in the open sea, then I had a lot more to master before I could call myself a sailor. I'd have to make my trips with more method, more science, and if I was to be able to make the crossing single-handed, then from now on I should almost always sail alone. A brave new world awaited.

I'd miss being with Adèle. I remembered how in the New-town river, we'd found free moorings by a ramshackle boat-yard far upstream in a creek. You had to tie the bow of the boat to a post on the bank and the stern to a special rope that stretched out from the bank into the river. It had taken us a while to figure that out, but we didn't care. We walked a mile in our sea boots and drank cold beer at a pub. We stole blackberries from an angry man's garden and caught up on sleep in a hay field. At night, swans passed us like merry-go-round sculptures and in the morning the mud jumped with tiny crabs. For a day and a night this was home and, when we were ready to leave, home left with us.

On another occasion, we'd sailed up the Beaulieu river on the Hampshire coast and run into a swarm of antique wooden dinghies, sailing frenetically and fast in every direction. Only later did we realize that we'd wandered into the starting line of a race, where the contestants were jockeying for position ahead of the starting horn. In the etiquette of dinghy racing, it turned out, we'd committed a major sin. In blissful ignor-ance, we just wondered how there could be so many people sailing similar boats at once and kept going. Further up the river, at a place called Gins, we tied up to a mooring buoy. This was a large floating rubber ball holding a thick rope which was in turn chained to the riverbed – all in all, about as secure as you could get and much better than an anchor. The knowledge made *Aquila* seem more comfortable than she'd ever been and when someone on shore played opera late into the night, the arias drifted over the river as clearly as if they'd been sung for us.

Then there'd been the day we were caught out by the weather at the end of a weekend sail to Wight. Once again we'd spent the night high up on the Newtown river, only to find on emerging the next day in the Solent that the weather had changed dramatically. The wind, which had been gentle the day before, beat frantically at Force 6. With all three reefs put into the main and our large foresail changed for the small jib, we began to tack back towards Keyhaven. The wind whipped up layer after layer of short, untidy waves. Spray, or rather big lumps of water, hit the boat, poured in, then sloshed about under the footboards. Never had we sailed in such conditions, yet we kept on, almost more out of ignorance than anything else.

Although we needed to cross over to the Hampshire coast in order to reach Keyhaven, we'd stuck to the Isle of Wight as long as we could. Each time we tried venturing out towards the middle of the Solent, the ferocity of the water sent *Aquila* pitching and rolling like a bronco. Then we'd turn back and keep working our way up the side of Wight, tacking close to the shore, where the waves and wind were more manageable. Our oilskins were soon dripping, our hair soaked, and we had almost to shout to communicate. Most worrying, *Aquila* was slowly but surely filling with water. Not another boat on the Solent, which at that time of year was usually crowded, could be seen. I remembered that somehow I found this encouraging, rather than frightening: pleasure boats were bound to keep away, but boats on a voyage, like *Aquila*, had to keep going.

Just past Yarmouth harbour on Wight a small beach appeared, where we pulled up to take stock and bail water out of the boat. We knew that from this point we could no longer postpone our crossing to the Hampshire side; any further up the coast of Wight and we'd run into the currents of the Trap and miss Keyhaven altogether. On the other hand, the water in the centre of the Solent looked terrifying. One patch was all white.

There was nothing for it. We had to cross, or be stranded on Wight for another night. Besides, there was a bloody-minded feeling that, having come this far, we must finish. We took down the jib to have even less sail to worry about and prepared to push off. Just then, a large man with thick daffodil-yellow hair approached. 'Are you OK?' he asked. I explained our predicament and we both looked out at the frothy sea. 'Would you like a tow? I've got a big powerboat in the harbour.' We thought about this for a second and declined. We acted on pride, but, as it turned out, we couldn't have made a better decision. Muttering prayers, we made a beeline for the Hampshire coast.

The tops of the waves reached well over the side of *Aquila* and it was a matter of steering so that we ran over and down the crests in order not to get swamped. Even so, occasionally we ran down into a trough so hard that the next wave broke right on the bow, soaking Adèle, who sat up forward, and burying all that admired woodwork under a blanket of solid water. Good God, I thought, so this is how you sink. It would have been no place for a tow – poor *Aquila* would probably have been pulled to pieces. At least under our own power, we could move as much as possible in harmony with the waves. With just the small mainsail up and as long as we both leaned far over the port side, the wind was manageable. Every so often gusts blew that I thought would flip *Aquila* over like an egg on the griddle, but on each occasion we survived. By the time we'd reached the far shore, water was again sloshing around the inside of *Aquila*, but we knew that we were only a short tack from Keyhaven and the voyage's end. We'd tamed a monster. Now, on return, I'd face these monsters alone.

My modern Gilliatt did exist – I found him in Jersey. Well, not entirely, but for a moment it did seem that the man from Hugo's pages had turned to flesh and blood. I'd been reading in the St Helier library about a local character from the nineteenth century named Philip Pinel, a wild Jerseyman who lived for decades in a cottage clinging to the Ecréhous reef in the sea north-east of Jersey. The Ecréhous covers a big area, but most of this is visible only at low water and at high tide, as if the Ecréhous were a hippo submerging himself bar the eyes and ears, the reef all but disappears. One of those parts usually remaining – and even this on occasions is threatened – is known as the Marmotière and it was here that Pinel built himself his simple stone cottage in 1848, just before Victor Hugo's arrival in the Channel Islands and eighteen years before the publication of *Les Travailleurs de la mer*.

Pinel, I thought, might well have been an inspiration for Hugo when he wrote the long part of *Les Travailleurs* that concerns Gilliatt's life on another reef, the Roches Douvres, while attempting to salvage Lethierry's wrecked ferry. Living on nothing but rain water, shellfish and ingenuity, and with only seagulls for company, Gilliatt seemed to share much with the life of the real castaway Philip Pinel. True, Pinel had a wife and enjoyed the occasional visits of fishermen, but just like Gilliatt he had almost no possessions, ate fish and bread baked in a home-made oven fuelled by seaweed, and drank rain water collected in a cistern. He became known as the king of the Ecréhous and in 1890 he made a basket from seaweed, filled it with fish and asked for the present to be sent to Queen Victoria. She sent in return a handsome blue coat.

Pinel, though, was not the last king of the Ecréhous, for in my own lifetime there had been another castaway, named Alphonse le Gastelois, and it was this man whom I took at first as the living embodiment of the fictional Gilliatt.

Alphonse le Gastelois lived on the reef from 1961 to 1975 in a rude stone cottage on the Marmotière, just like Pinel. His stay was fourteen years to the original king's fifty, but unlike Pinel, le Gastelois never had a wife to help. From old press clippings I understood that many people considered le Gastelois an unsavoury character who did not deserve to be humoured with the title of king. My hunch, though, was that he had been no more rough than Pinel but had not yet benefited from the softening effects of the passage of time. He'd left school at fourteen to become a farm labourer and fisherman, but was said to possess considerable natural intelligence. He was described as a loner and an eccentric, but that was hardly surprising for someone who lived alone on a reef, subsisting much as Pinel had done a century before. He ate shellfish, seaweed and food left or brought by visiting yachtsmen. He drank rain water. His chief vice was the chewing of tobacco. He studied the tides, read the Bible, kept contact with passing fishermen and wrote energetically, though not necessarily clearly, in defence of his claim to ownership of the Ecréhous. In a newspaper photograph taken well into his island sojourn, his overcoat is in tatters and held around the waist with string. In another, he is carrying his wooden dinghy on his back, tortoise-style. Le Gastelois looks extremely happy.

So here was a late-twentieth-century Gilliatt, stranded on his rock, where, as Hugo said, 'to obtain water was the first problem; how to procure food the second; where to sleep the third'. Gilliatt, of course, had things worse than le Gastelois, but the similarities were remarkable. Le Gastelois resembled Hugo's character in that he was not only a 'poor fisher of crayfish and crabs' but also an outsider for whom the rock was a place of refuge in an unfriendly world.

In the fictional case, superstition made people ostracize Gilliatt; in the case of Alphonse le Gastelois it was mob justice. Wrongly suspected by the police of a series of rapes and molestations of children in the Jersey countryside in the 1960s, le Gastelois literally went into exile, becoming the king and sole subject of the one place in the Channel Islands where he was sure not to be harassed. People hadn't liked him because he dressed shabbily, lived in a run-down cottage and muttered to himself, but he had done nothing wrong. Unfortunately for le Gastelois, the police took a decade to catch the real criminal. Expecting to be on the Ecréhous just long enough to get out of the limelight, he ended up there for fourteen years. An extraordinary fate, but perhaps only a more extreme version of that combination of freedom and imprisonment meeting all those who take to the sea. The sailor enjoys the liberty of open spaces and an empty horizon, yet, like le Gastelois on his island, he can never leave the tiny cocoon of his boat. The same applies to lighthouse keepers, to fishermen and indeed to anyone whose business is among the waves. The paradox, after all, lies at the root of the whole identity of the British Isles, and, therefore, of the Channel – that narrow sea which for some is a wall, for others a door.

Several people, including a lawyer who'd known him, told me that Alphonse le Gastelois was dead. Certainly no one had heard of him for years and the library's thick file of press clippings dried up in the early 1980s. In my hotel, I sat down with the telephone directory and began to leaf through. Jersey's Norman roots jumped out from every page. My finger ran down the columns: le, le, le. Then, to my amazement, le Gastelois . . . A. le Gastelois, Devonshire Cottage, St Helier. I dialled. There was an answer.

'Hello, is this Alphonse le Gastelois, the king of the Ecréhous?'

Breathing. Then, 'I'm the one.'

'I'm very interested in your story. Would there be any chance of meeting?'

Breathing, this time for twenty, twenty-five, thirty seconds. 'I don't feel well.'

'Yes, but . . .'

'At 2 p.m.'

'OK, I'll . . .'

The phone had gone dead.

The king of the Ecréhous's abode was at the end of an alley, more shack than cottage. It had two rooms. In the first, plastic bags and boxes were piled almost as high as the ceiling. Alphonse le Gastelois lived in the other, most of which was also taken up with plastic bags and boxes. He sat on a small bed next to a tower of ten old telephone directories. I remembered how many rings there'd been after I'd dialled and wondered how often he used the phone. A white beard ran down his chest. Yellow fingernails stuck out by a centimetre. He had pale blue eyes. He wore several jerseys, a blue coat, a floppy woollen hat and glasses that were held together with thick tape. He said he was eighty-six. His smell was overpowering. When he removed a double layer of socks to show me sores he said had been caused by the French nuclear power station on Cap de la Hague, I was afraid I'd choke.

'How are you feeling?' I asked.

He pointed at the ground. 'I'm waiting for that.'

I asked what life had been like on the Ecréhous. 'Fourteen years on a bare rock. I was better out there. As you see around here, there's dog shit everywhere.' Was it hard in winter? 'For three months I wouldn't see anyone. There were some fishermen who'd come and I had a little dinghy that you could put a mast in. I used to carry it on my back and drop it into the water. I could collect anyone off their boats and bring them ashore. I'd wait on the headland and see if there were any sailing boats. Then I'd wonder if they were coming this way.' What had he eaten? 'You could find the odd lobster. Not in the day, but at night it was there for the taking. You'd shine a torch and you'd take a stick like that with a conger hook on the end and just spear it.'

Our discussion was not easy, for the king's mind swung this way and that, and although for one moment he might make perfect sense, he raved the next. Trying to keep him on the subject of the Ecréhous, I asked what he'd done all day on his own.

'Think, mostly.' What about? 'Mischief.'

I laughed, almost forgetting the smell, because Alphonse was chuckling too and for a second we seemed to connect. I asked about the first king. 'The old king of the Ecréhous, he liked the French and got on with them,' Alphonse le Gastelois said. 'So do I. The old king, if we'd met, we'd have argued, but we probably would have got on.' Then, ejecting a tape from a prehistoric cassette player, he shoved in another and pressed the huge P L A Y button. Out filtered a frail voice – his own.

> 'And it made me sad to hear her sing.
> Then I wonder, yes I wonder,
> will the angels appear yonder,
> will the angels bring their harps . . .'

For the first time, it occurred to me that apart from his fourteen years on the reef and his miserable life alone in St Helier, there must have been a time when Alphonse le Gastelois had friends, when he loved and was loved.

Motioning at me to wait where I was (there was nowhere I could have moved), the old man lurched into a mountain of old suitcases and shopping bags. Out came a black box containing several books. Le Gastelois, adjusting his broken glasses, began to read, or rather mumble, flipping from one page to another, then changing books, starting again, before taking up yet another book. I understood little, but I could see the titles: there were law books, constitutions, acts of Parliament, charters . . . It was time for me to leave.

Le Gastelois raised his eyes as soon as I moved. 'You're not the relation of the bloody wandering Jew, are you?'

'Alphonse,' I said as I got up, 'I was just wondering – do you still go to the sea?'

'I can't move. Only as far as the street,' he replied.

'When was the last time you saw the sea?'

'Oh, I don't remember.'

The old king looked very sad.

★

Walking away along the sea front, my thoughts returned to Gilliatt. Le Gastelois didn't have his character. Gilliatt was never garrulous and, had he lived to be old, I doubted whether he would ever have gone to pieces quite so badly, whatever his fortunes. But I'd found a part of Gilliatt, or at least a part of his story, in among those rubbish bags and boxes, just as I'd found a little of the rest of the book everywhere else I went in the islands. The missing piece though – and the one I needed most, for it was this that might help me in my journey – was Gilliatt the sailor, the man who could read the water. After all, it was in his honour that I'd named, or half-named, my boat.

Back at the hotel, I got talking about le Gastelois and the Ecréhous with the Portuguese man on the front desk, whom I liked at once because he offered me an espresso and because his accent and mannerisms brought light into what was an otherwise stolidly English hotel lobby. The Ecréhous were famous among people in Jersey, he said, but if I wanted to meet someone who really knew the rocks, I should phone this man. He wrote down a number and a name on a scrap of paper. 'Frank Lawrence. He knows everything there.'

Frank Lawrence was my missing piece. He lived with his wife in the woods in the centre of Jersey, but he kept a tiny dinghy in the back of his car the way land people keep a pair of boots. At sixty-eight he looked as strong as a walrus and his skin was clear and smooth. There was nothing he hadn't done at sea. He started with his father on an Icelandic trawler, maintained the buoys and beacons around the island, crisscrossed the world in merchant ships, plied the English Channel with British Rail ships, ran the Jersey pilot boat and served as second coxswain on the St Helier lifeboat. One of his sons had taken over as Jersey pilot. 'That's the way it's always been.' He showed me a family scrapbook crammed with newspaper clippings about relatives and pictures of boats and men in oilskins.

When he worked on the buoys and beacons, learning the passages and traps of the Ecréhous and Minquiers was his job. He'd wait until low water, when the rock teeth were bared, and jump around marking the territory with little more than wooden poles. By the time Frank became a pilot, no one could guide ships better, and if he'd been on the bridge of Lethierry's ferry in *Les Travailleurs*, just as if Gilliatt had been, there would have been no wreck. Even now in his retirement, Frank could not let go of that hidden world he knew so well. Working from a small room in his house, he was building folios of computerized sea charts backed up by photographs of the area and navigational instructions that appeared at the click of the mouse. 'I've gone from planting sticks to computers,' he said, smiling.

I told Frank of my plans – that I wanted to cross the Channel in my dinghy, that I wanted to be a sailor. What did he advise? 'Some people are natural seamen more than others, handling a boat, looking at weather. I can always tell one by the way they pick up a rope. I'd say that my second son is a natural seaman.'

So what were the most important things to learn? 'You've got a lot to sort out. There're the tides for starters.' Yes, I said, the tides, and I admitted that I did not have a good grip on tides at all, and even told him about my aborted swim from Sark to Brecqhou. 'You've really got to know that. Currents go one way and then another. That determines your route, especially in the Channel. The Channel acts like a funnel and you get really big tides. The Channel can be very, very dangerous. Then there's the wind. If you go in a light wind, you'll go very slow. If you go in a good wind, there'll be more of a sea. If wind is against tide, you'll get rough seas. If you cross in a wide part of the Channel, you're longer at sea. If you cross at Dover, you'll get an awful lot of shipping.'

I gave a despairing laugh. So what should I concentrate on?

Frank didn't hesitate. To progress beyond short hops, I needed to know the workings of the sea – the tides, the waves, the winds and movement of ships. Only then would I understand how to get a boat from one place to another. 'You need to learn navigation first and foremost,' he said. 'If I were you, I'd get going with that right away.' Gilliatt the navigator indeed.

My mind in a whirl, I thanked him and left.

4

The Solent, white with yachts in summer, was deserted in winter. Light, glancing off the empty water from the low sun, became metallic and chilled. Sound – the sound of water against the boat, the sound of the wind, even silence – became brittle. Many large boats and dinghies had been taken out of the water for repairs and storage that would last until May. Even the boats still afloat rarely set sail, left lifeless in back creeks and marinas, their hatches locked, their sails removed. Often, apart from the ferries to the Isle of Wight, *Aquila-Gilliatt* (as I now called her from time to time) was about the only boat on the Solent, while more than five yachts sailing at any one time meant a busy day. The effect of this was to make the Solent appear much bigger. Maybe that was also the result of the shorter days, which meant that what should have been a leisurely cruise became a race against the dark.

In summer, a day's sail often ended with a swim and time to dry off. From November the sea was losing heat by the day and by January it chilled to the bone. For the first time I began to wear gloves and a woolly hat. But capsizing, especially far from shore, would spell trouble. Crippled by hypothermia, one might not be able to right the boat, one might capsize a second time or simply freeze afterwards. So I invested in a dry suit, a lightweight, one-piece rubber suit with sealed neck, feet and wrists that was impervious, meaning that in an accident I would stay dry, a possibly life-saving factor. I also learned to tie myself in, a simple rope around my waist and the other end attached to *Aquila* so that if I ever fell overboard we'd not be separated. These were no longer the conditions for long swims, especially now that I was almost always alone, with no Adèle to stop and turn the boat. One of my sailing guides contained a table showing that in the Channel in February survival time after falling overboard was thirty minutes, while numbness and loss of coordination, conditions themselves that could lead to something more serious, would strike much earlier.

People seeing me alone on the water often expressed disbelief. The harbour master of Keyhaven, motoring past one morning as I was getting *Aquila* ready to leave Hurst: 'Are you OK?' A sailor in a dinghy with a red sail racing past my anchorage in drizzle on the Newtown river: 'Are you OK?' The crew of a yacht picking up a mooring next to mine in the Beaulieu river as I worked to get the boat tent up before dark: 'Are you OK?' But, perversely, I welcomed the winter. In fact I wanted the sea colder, the wind harder and waves higher. Partly this was for practical reasons: I thought that the worse the conditions, the more I'd be forced to learn. But there was also another reason. The difficulties of sailing in winter, I felt, would allow me to begin paying the dues that I knew in my heart were owed – owed to the sea and owed to the real sailors, the Frank Lawrences and Gilliatts, for whom the sea was truly the giver and taker of life. I'd presumed to join them with only the shortest of apprenticeships, so now was the time to take some blows. The last of my illusions must fall. Only then might the sea, in its infinite, ceaselessly changing character, be revealed.

Shortly after returning from the Channel Islands in November I went out to the Trap with Adèle. She wanted to see the place for herself, while I wanted to pick up where I'd left off. I felt haunted by my swim in the Gouliot and by the words of Frank Lawrence, 'The Channel can be very, very dangerous.' It seemed to me that the Trap was a good place to begin facing reality.

Inexplicably, that day barely a ripple disturbed the Trap. One patch made a half-hearted attempt at those messy triangular waves and the current was still there, sweeping up past Hurst Castle into the expanse of Christchurch bay, but we saw none of the mayhem. When we returned with the change of the tide later, the water had become a little more wild. *Aquila*, with the south-west wind behind her, surfed down the wave fronts, smooth as a toboggan. Still, there was nothing to remind one of the Trap of the past. Adèle hardly believed in the beast at all.

Soon after, and this time alone, I returned. The lure of the open sea – the thrill of bursting from the Trap into water where the southern horizon ended in nothing but an empty curve – was too strong to resist. Besides, the last time had been too easy; I had unfinished business.

On this occasion the sea was somewhere between the state of my two previous visits, probably what the weather forecasters would call 'slight to moderate'. Once more I rushed through, *Aquila* dipping into troughs, then popping back up for air and diving down once more. I sailed out into the open bay, picking my way as best I could between waves, though occasionally taking a bucketful over the bows. Satisfied that everything was handling well, I turned to get back into the Solent.

Now, of course, the only way to pass the Trap under sail is using the tide. I still didn't know much about tides, but the basics were obvious: you left the Solent out of the Trap on the outgoing, or ebb, tide, then returned at leisure during the subsequent six hours of incoming, or flood, tide. On this day, though, the incoming tide took place all the morning, meaning I couldn't get out of the Solent. Then the ebb tide lasted all afternoon, meaning I wouldn't be able to get back in, as only after dark would the tide switch again to incoming. But in my hunger to deal with the Trap, I made a gamble. Between two tides, as I'd heard Philip say on Sark, there was something called slack water, a short period when there was almost no current at all. I'd rather have been able to go out and return a few hours later, but even a quick trip would help me get my fix of the open sea, so, provided there were no delays, why shouldn't I be able to nip out and then back in during the slack?

At first it seemed that my plan had been perfect. Not only had I got out without difficulty, but the ride back into the Solent was proceeding just as well. *Aquila* sailed smartly along the beach towards Hurst Castle and entered the narrows. I rejoiced. Then about halfway around the curve of the castle, within a stone's throw of the Solent, she stopped dead. The wind still blew, the sails were full, but the boat would not move forward, held back by an invisible force – the current, damn it, the current had begun flowing out of the Solent. Whatever I'd thought, either the slack period didn't exist or I'd got my timing wrong. For all I knew, I might even have left the Solent not during slack but rather during the first stages of the ebb. There was no slack now, for sure; this was the ebb. As *Aquila* hovered between wind and tide, I could see and feel the sea gallop past. Rocks and poles under the castle wall were awash. The Trap had shut. There was no choice. I turned *Aquila* and sailed back with the current into the open sea.

146

From an initial panic came anger, and from that a determination that fed something mad. The next flood tide to take me through would not be until dusk and I didn't want to wait that long. I'd never sailed in the dark and besides I was cold and increasingly angry. I had to find a way through. The Trap must not win. As soon as this was decided, I turned *Aquila* and made a second run, but again she stalled in that place by the castle. The current was building and the surface of the sea had become agitated. *Aquila* rose and fell on the waves like a leaf in the wind. I turned her into an angle away from the castle, towards the other side of the Trap. Maybe by picking up speed and testing different areas I'd find a way through. We progressed, and for a few seconds I thought we'd make it, but whenever I reached a certain line, up came that invisible barrier and we made no further ground. The waves in the centre were especially violent. *Aquila* was taking a terrific knocking and for the first time I thought I might capsize. If that happened, I knew that I might never right her – not in this tumult. I'd be swept right out to the Needles. Out of nowhere, fear moved in. I realized now that with one bad mistake I could be wrecked.

All I had to do was sail over by one of the beaches, drop anchor and wait until the tide turned that night, but I wouldn't give in. Driven beyond common sense, I now took *Aquila* back to that spot by the castle, stalled again, but instead of turning away edged right up to the shingle spit coming from the castle wall and leapt out on to land. If I couldn't sail *Aquila* round the point, I'd drag her. The Trap would not win.

The current swirling around my legs reminded me of the Gouliot. This was a river, not a sea. For the first ten metres or so, I made steady progress, taking care not to lose my footing, for that would surely mean being carried away. Equally, I had to concentrate on not losing my grip on the painter of the boat, for then she too would be carried away on the flow, God only knew where. Two obstacles lay in my path. The first were large rocks under the water, which helped me get a purchase with my feet but, as I increasingly realized, posed a terrible threat to *Aquila*. The second were huge thick wooden pilings driven into the ground in rows to halt the erosion of the shingle spit. The spaces between each pillar were just too narrow for me to pull *Aquila* through, meaning that I had to wade out as far as the last pillar and pull the boat around. The effort was exhausting, for to reach the furthest pillar meant going into water up to my chest, strengthening the effect of the currents and weakening my footing. Holding with one arm on to each pillar and with the other on to *Aquila*, I managed to get around the first row of pilings. After that, there were at least three more rows to round, but in terms of distance I was halfway around the spit. The Trap would *not* win.

The second row of pilings extended even further into the deep than the last. I was up to my neck in water, one leg and arm wrapped around a post, the other leg braced against a boulder and my other arm fighting not to drag *Aquila* around but simply to keep her in check against the current, which, because we were rounding the corner, had got stronger. Tourists at the castle were beginning to gather and watch. 'Are you OK?' came the inevitable question. 'Yes, yes, just fine.' I tried to smile, although I felt desperate. 'Do you want me to call the coastguard?' asked a man. 'I'm affiliated. They could be here in minutes if I call on my mobile.' I was in a fury, dry in my special suit, but simultaneously cold and sweating. One hand was bleeding. 'No, no, really, I'm absolutely fine,' I answered. By now I'd managed to squeeze myself past the second row of posts, but *Aquila*, dragged all the time by that current, was never going to follow. The current was relentless, pulling, pulling, and punishing any slip.

'You'll never make it,' a woman said. She appeared with a man and a dog right on the shingle near me. 'That current's running at full strength. There's no way to pull your boat around.' The woman said this so calmly, so softly, that in an instant my resolve crumbled. I'd been defeated. 'You're right,' I said. Ahead of me were another two rows of pilings. This wouldn't work. Thinking now only of saving *Aquila* from damage against the pilings or rocks, I steadied her, jumped aboard, seized the tiller and steered away from the cursed shore and back into the open sea. The Trap had won.

That afternoon, while I waited for the tide to change, I sailed far down the beaches of Christchurch bay, fighting the cold, which had numbed my feet and hands, and asking both *Aquila* and the Trap for forgiveness. The Trap had won and always would win. A good head, not brute strength, prevailed at sea. I had only to think of Gilliatt to know that. The sea set the rules and they were the only ones that mattered. When I got back – if I got back – I would study those tides and all that went with them. The fury was now burnt out, the humiliation turned to repentance, and, strangely enough, I felt in enormously high spirits. I wanted to know the sea. Well, here it was.

At sunset, around the time the incoming tide started, I headed back to the Trap. The wind had dropped and I glided through past the castle, past the scene of that struggle, with barely a sound. The sun hit the horizon, the moon switched on and stars, in their thousands, fell from the sky like loose change. For forty-five minutes I sailed across the Solent to Lymington on a sea so smooth that the heavens were reflected and the two great surfaces became one. Finding my way in the dark was not at all as hard as I'd feared, for I'd sailed this part of the Solent so many times now that it was no different from crossing a familiar park at night. I'd never been so content on *Aquila* – so content that at first I didn't realize that I'd begun to shiver.

As I floated up to the slipway deep in Lymington harbour, my new base for the winter, a motor launch pulled alongside. On her hull was written POLICE. 'Are you the boat that was out by Hurst Castle just now?' called a man. 'That's right.' I chuckled. 'Everything OK then?' I answered yes. Having reached the slipway now, I jumped out, giving silent thanks for the feel of land under my boots. The police boat, meanwhile, had docked at the nearby pontoon. 'Are you the owner of that boat, sir?' the man said. 'We do have to check.' I asked why. 'Because boats go missing.' There was no need to check this one, I said. 'Well, this is a rather unusual time to be sailing a dinghy,' the policeman answered more firmly. 'Do you have any proof of identity on you?' At first I'd thought the police were simply checking I was in one piece, but now I saw they suspected me. I looked at the policeman in disbelief, then smiled to myself. This man would help me pull *Aquila-Gilliatt*, laden down with camping gear as she was, out of the water. After that, I'd show him my ID.

Now I remembered. During that sail through the dark from Hurst to Lymington, there had been one fast boat that went past. She was some way off, close to the Isle of Wight and moving in the direction I'd just come from. All that had been visible were the green and red starboard and port lights on the bow and a white light above, but I was sure now that that had been the police boat. In other words, they hadn't just run into me in Lymington harbour by chance. They'd gone out looking for me, but because I was carrying no lights and had been sailing in the more shallow part of the Solent they had shot right past. Only on return had they had the chance to find me in the harbour. At least that's what I reckoned. Which meant that someone out there by the Trap had seen me and called the authorities. I recalled several lone figures I'd seen walking the beaches; probably one of them made the call. At first I supposed that somebody was simply concerned about my safety, but when it became clear the police were more interested in what I was up to out in the dark, I wondered whether in fact I hadn't been turned in by one of their spies.

Principally to prevent smuggling, the police and Customs maintained a network of informers along the coast. The south coast, with hundreds of coves or, as beyond the Trap, long, desolate beaches, was perfect for smuggling. A fast motorboat could cross to France and back in a couple of hours, its low profile not even registering on the coastguard's radar screens. A yacht that didn't appear to be anything other than one of the hundreds of pleasure boats threading the Channel could anchor offshore and use its dinghy to deliver drugs from as far as North Africa or the Caribbean. The authorities couldn't possibly watch all that coastline and so they tried to encourage locals to watch for anything unusual – four-wheel-drive cars on beaches at night, landings by small boats at odd places, flights by light aircraft not showing lights. In Cornwall, a fishing boat had recently helped the coastguard intercept a yacht which attracted suspicion because of the skipper's reluctance to find shelter from a storm. It turned out to be carrying 2.65 tons of cannabis.

In the past, it was difficult to recruit citizen spies because many living onshore had as much to fear, and as much to gain, from the smugglers as they did from the authorities. 'In some parts of the maritime counties, the whole people are so generally engaged on smuggling that it is impossible to find a jury that will, upon trial, do justice to an officer of the revenue in any case whatsoever,' Parliament heard in 1736. Rudyard Kipling was not being entirely fanciful in his 'A Smuggler's Song', where he warned:

> If you wake at Midnight, and hear a horse's feet,
> Don't go drawing back the blind, or looking in the street,
> Them that asks no questions isn't told a lie.
> Watch the wall, my darling, while the Gentlemen go by!
> Five and twenty ponies
> Trotting through the dark –
> Brandy for the Parson,
> 'Baccy for the Clerk;
> Laces for a lady, letters for a spy,
> Watch the wall, my darling, while the Gentlemen go by!
> . . . If you do as you've been told, likely there's a chance,
> You'll be given a dainty doll, all the way from France,
> With a cap of pretty lace, and a velvet hood –
> A present from the Gentlemen, along o' being good!

I had to admit that the thought I might have been mistaken for a trafficker gave me a thrill. Ever since going on the open sea I'd discovered a sensation of illicit pleasure in being out there alone in my tiny, noiseless boat. A Wayfarer wasn't an obvious choice for smuggling these days, but in times past it might have been excellent for certain jobs: a good sea boat and easily hidden.

Before motors, the smuggler had to be first a sailor and only then a criminal. The West Country smuggler, in particular, had to be a good mariner, for he faced a tougher crossing than his counterparts in Kent and Sussex. Not only were Brittany and the Channel Islands a good twenty-four hours' sail away, but the coasts on both sides were exceptionally rocky. Survival required expert knowledge of the coastal conditions and currents, while only the truly intrepid could hope to do well. Despite the great dangers of exposing an open boat to the crossing, some Cornish even mimicked the Kent smugglers in their use of long, narrow rowing boats. Ideally suited for a fast crossing between Dungeness and Boulogne, these galleys could outrun pursuing coastguard cutters by rowing directly into the wind, at which the cutter, having to tack, would fall behind.

Harry Carter, a Cornishman born in Prussia Cove, near Penzance, in 1749, belonged to such a family of sailor outlaws. Not interested in petty trade, they ran large, heavily armed boats and operated their business with a strict code of honour. The head of the family firm, John Carter, or 'the King of Prussia', as he was known, was renowned for having raided an official warehouse only to retrieve his own goods, not to loot the rest of the stores. This was not unusual in the Western Approaches. In 1770, a traveller was amazed to witness the captain of a ship returning from Asia to England accept a banker's cheque for £1,224 from a tea smuggler. 'These people always deal with the strictest honour. If they did not, their business would cease,' the captain said.

Carter was a thief of such peculiar honour that he gave up his violent ways and converted to Methodism. Having swapped his pistols for a Bible, the one-time brigand set about his home village near Newlyn preaching, managing on several occasions to work his large congregations into religious frenzies. There may have been some who disapproved of his past, but more likely the Cornish forgave him, partly because he preached well and partly because smuggling was not widely seen as entirely evil – it involved, after all, a dangerous life at sea. It was the inheritors of this Cornish Methodism whom I'd met at the Fishermen's Mission back in Newlyn, a much reduced band, but still full of passion and still with one foot in the sea. Certainly the old sailor delivering the sermon had had the same rhetorical skills ascribed to Harry Carter. I could think only that Carter and his ilk proved that strong faith is to be found in the sea.

At about the same time a very different set of people ran the smuggling at the eastern end of the Channel, land-based mobsters with none of the saving graces of a sailor like Harry Carter, relying instead on their ability to sow fear among locals and Customs men alike. The most notorious was the Hawkhurst gang, which worked all along the route of the trip I'd taken from Bognor, especially in the marshes around Dungeness and the villages a little further inland.

The Hawkhurst gang didn't hesitate before shooting or beating to death various law-enforcement men and for years they were untouchable, able to swagger into their favourite drinking den, the Mermaid Inn at Rye, with loaded pistols and other weapons, and to extort goods and money from any village they pleased. The authorities were helpless. Until, that is, in April 1747, when one village, Goudhurst, decided to put up a fight. William Sturt, a local man who'd recently retired from the army, set about training a militia from the men in the village. When the Hawkhurst leader, Thomas Kingsmill, caught wind of this defiance, he gathered his toughs and rode into Goudhurst, intending to teach the villagers a lesson. Sturt and his men, hidden in all the strategic points of the village centre – the medieval church tower, the pub standing over a sharp street corner – were waiting. This was the account in the *Maidstone Journal* published on the centenary of the event on 27 April 1847:

[The Hawkhurst men] entered town on horseback, bodies bared to the waist, armed with blunderbusses, carbines and hangers [short swords]. Kingsmill swore he had killed and been at the death of 50 Custom House officers and he would 'broyl four of the townsmen's hearts for supper'. The inhabitants were in their houses when Kingsmill commenced the attack riding to the Star and Crown Inn door and rearing his horse to force it, when a person from an upper window fired and knocked him from his horse lifeless; another desperate ruffian Borent Woollet, while leaping his horse over the churchyard fence exclaimed, 'Shoot and be . . .' and was shot from the church tower.

Today, smuggling is as pervasive as it was at the time of the Hawkhurst gang and the basic causes are the same: the Channel separates two markets with greatly varying tax rates and prices on popular goods; the Channel is just narrow enough to be crossed in small boats and just wide enough to make life difficult for the authorities. Except for drugs, even the cargoes being smuggled are similar. In the eighteenth century, tea, tobacco, brandy and luxury French cloth were the prime illegal imports, while today the list is topped by tobacco, spirits and beer. Because of the European single market, the lines between smuggling and legal imports have, if anything, become more blurred, making the Customs officials' jobs all the harder. The British national pastime of a 'booze cruise' to Calais hypermarkets is especially complex to police, since provided that travellers can show their cargo is for personal use, not resale, no restrictions apply. In other words, the individual, no longer dependent on highly taxed British goods, gets away with legalized smuggling. Meanwhile, real smugglers, intending to sell the French- or Belgian-bought goods at huge mark-ups in Britain, pose, often successfully, as innocent day-trippers.

'We have to determine whether the goods are truly intended for personal use,' one of the Customs officers, Nigel Knott, told me during a visit to Dover. 'They'll say anything sometimes. We've heard it all. You hear they've bought an entire van-load of tobacco for warming houses, as compost for the bean trench, for bathing to cure lumbago . . . We had one group explaining their load by saying that they wanted to hand out 200 cigarettes to everyone at a wedding. Sometimes they make it easy for us. If a person with an entire van of cigarettes tells you that it's for their personal use and you work out it would take them three and a half years longer to smoke the cigarettes than the shelf life on the packets, then you're suspicious. Another guy admitted in an unguarded moment that he personally didn't smoke.' But apart from dead give-aways, Customs officers rely only on profiles of potential malefactors who can then be plucked from the crowd. 'We're really just professional people watchers,' Knott said.

At the docks, HM Customs and Excise had a warehouse

stacked to the roof with Stolitsa vodka, Abbaye Saint-Laurent wine, Regal, Superkings and Viceroy cigarettes. The mountain grew by the hour as forklift trucks stacked newly impounded crates. The contents of this trophy room were all destined for destruction – cigarettes incinerated, wines and spirits converted into industrial alcohol, the beer into shampoo and animal feed, the glass for recycling. But whatever Customs, with its sniffer dogs, X-ray machines, fibre-optic cameras, fast boats, Jeeps and spies, managed to haul in, a whole lot more would get past. Every twenty minutes another ferry docked in Dover, hundreds more cars and lorries rolled down the ramps, another long line of faces paraded past. Roughly 25,000 passengers enter every day and some of them are bound to be smugglers. Only a very, very few are ever caught.

A person able to bring in a kilo of cocaine, the size of a bag of sugar, will be well rewarded, but there is also good money to be made in the smuggling of tobacco and alcohol, with far lower risks of serious prison sentences than those facing dealers in illegal narcotics. In Belgium rolling tobacco cost £1.85 for 50 grams, while in Britain taxes made the same weed cost £7.50. When the duty on a pint of beer was four pence in France, it was thirty-three pence in Britain. The figures were not much different from those exploited by the smugglers of the eighteenth century, when tea cost three pence a pound in France and twenty-five pence in England. Smuggling paid.

'People still want to take the risk. We'll never really know if we're doing better or not, because we're dealing with unreported crime. It's an enigma,' Knott said. Before us stretched the amazing sight of a million cigarettes laid out in cartons along the false floor of a smuggler's truck that had just been pulled in. It was clear that cross-Channel smugglers were not easily deterred. 'We've had heroin in cans of Guinness; drugs hidden in inner tubes. Also had it in a carving of three monkeys. We've had a domino set made out of cocaine, Ecstasy tablets in a truckload of milk cartons, cocaine inside a pair of avocados, amphetamines hidden inside platform shoes.' Knott liked to crack jokes about these tricks, but the longer we toured the cinder-block buildings, warehouses, concrete ramps and traffic cones, the grim machinery of Customs' attempt to filter the bad from the good, the more his cracks seemed only to mask distaste and fear.

'Somehow through fiction and the unpopularity of governments, smuggling has been romanticized. But it's gang warfare. It's murderers and thugs,' he said. 'The bootleggers are drifting into criminal gangs now, getting organized the same way as drug smuggling. There's a hierarchy. You get the van driver who actually makes the crossing. Sometimes he'll be accompanied by a granny to look less suspicious. Then you get the enforcer, the foreman who manages and guards the stuff while the drivers are on their way again. This takes place in car parks and around Dover. You know, many officers would rather have to deal with drug smugglers than these bootleggers. Drug smugglers know the risks, but they don't offer the same level of immediate violence and abuse as the bootleggers. About 80 per cent of these people have a criminal record for violence.'

Knott offered to take me around the hovercraft terminal, where we'd be certain to spot some of the bootleggers. We were in a four-wheel-drive car with HM Customs and Excise and the coat of arms emblazoned on the bonnet. 'Usually we wouldn't go in a high-profile car like this. We'll just swing by to give them a scare.' We entered the car park and passed the main entrance to the terminal. 'Look, that's them.' Half a dozen large men with shaved heads stood on the pavement drinking pints of beer and talking on mobile phones. They didn't look scared.

Still bruised from my battering in the Trap, I went home from the Solent with just one aim: to get to grips with the whole question of currents and tides. I piled the following on my desk: the *RYA Book of Navigation*, *Britain and the British Seas* by Sir Halford J. Mackinder, a booklet called *Solent Tides*, the navigational *Channel Pilot* and Caesar's *The Gallic War*. For luck, I threw in the *Beginner's Guide* – it was always worth re-reading. Then, I sat down and began to learn.

Sir Halford J. Mackinder laid out how tides are 'generated in abysmal waters by lunar and solar influence'. The moon and to a lesser extent the sun pull on the Earth, literally raising a bulge of ocean on two opposite sides of the world. Each bulge is high water, while the parts of ocean dragged away to create those bulges are at low water. As the Earth spins, the focus of this gravitational pull moves, giving any particular spot a high tide and a low tide every six or so hours later. So regular are these movements that, according to my *Beginner's Guide*, people used to believe 'tides were the respirations of a huge sea monster'.

In very deep open water, the rise and fall of the tide is often only about a metre, while in the bottleneck of the Channel it can reach eleven metres. 'The crest of a vast but imperceptible wave passes at several hundred miles an hour in deep oceans,' Mackinder explained. Then, approaching Britain from the Atlantic, this tidal wave hits the continental shelf, reduces speed sharply and so begins to well up. Caught between the coasts of England and France, that original tidal wave is compressed even more. Looking for escape, huge quantities of water attack in every possible direction, flooding estuaries, harbours, beaches and marshes. That means not only huge rises and falls in water levels in harbours and on beaches, but also a terrific increase in currents, compared to the relatively benign currents of the open ocean. At certain choke points of the Channel, such as the gap between Alderney and France, the tide can tear along at up to eight knots, or nautical miles, an hour – enough to send anything but powerful motorboats and ships backwards. Around promontories such as Portland Bill or Beachy Head, the water is also trapped, then released in a frenzied stream. As the *Channel Pilot* said, 'In the Channel, the tide is king.'

When Caesar crossed the Channel the first time, arriving in Kent the morning of 26 August 55 BC, his men secured a bridgehead while their ships were beached or anchored close by the shore. Four days later, a storm blew up, scattering reinforcements that had been about to land, and also causing havoc among the ships already there, a calamity which severely damaged the legions' principal way of escape. Not only the storm was to blame, but also the powerful tide that day, which, unlike the weather, would have been easy to predict. Caesar wrote:

As it happened there was a full moon that night. On this day the Ocean tides are usually at their highest – a fact of which our men were unaware. So at one and the same time the tide had flooded the warships by which Caesar had the army ferried across . . . Nor did our men get any chance to manoeuvre them or bring them assistance. Several of the ships were wrecked, the rest had lost their ropes, their anchors, and the rest of their rigging, and were unfit to sail. The inevitable result was panic throughout the army. For there were no other ships to transport them back.

There is almost no tidal action in the Mediterranean and most Romans knew nothing of these matters. While Caesar must have noticed the draining and filling of his harbour at Boulogne, in his comment about the full moon he betrayed his ignorance about one of the most basic details, one that I too was only just coming to understand.

At full moon, and also new moon, the sun, Earth and moon are aligned, making the gravitational pull that is at the origin of all tides vastly more powerful than at times of half-moon, when the sun, Earth and moon are at angles to each other. These full- and new-moon tides, which bring the sea higher up beaches and induce stronger currents, are called 'spring' tides, while the comparatively gentle half-moon tides are 'neaps', from the Old English, meaning 'without power of advancing'. So, when the storm hit Caesar's fleet at the end of August, not only would the shore waters have been deeper than during the previous week but the currents would also have been more violent. After failing to take proper care over the berthing of his ships, it was predictable that in a storm those at anchor would be pulled free and those thought safely on dry land would soon be awash.

At almost every word I read, I gave a mental thump on the table and thought, But of course! So many scenes I had witnessed only now began to make sense. The times when the water in an anchorage dropped to bewilderingly low levels, when the plug seemed to have been pulled out of the seabed

– these were at spring tides. The times when the current ran so hard that in trying to cross the Solent in *Aquila* I'd make as much ground sideways as forwards – that was the current of a spring tide. Now I thought of it, I'd even seen the perfect alignment one evening of the setting sun in the west and the rising full moon in the east. No wonder that the Beaulieu river had that night drained and flooded so much every six hours that one could scarcely believe one was still moored in the same place. No wonder, too, that in the Gouliot I'd almost been swept out to sea: I'd been swimming in one of the most brutal passages of the Channel and if I looked back into my diary I could see that this had been at around the time of the new moon. As for my escapades in the Trap, the mystery was over. In *Solent Tides*, which was an atlas using arrows to show the strength and direction of the tidal current, the Trap was marked at one stage with a spring current of 4.5 knots.

From then I was able to use the tide, that breathing of the ocean, to my advantage. Never again did I have to sail as blindly as Caesar. Awareness of whether the tide was on the flood or ebb, in other words going east down the Solent or west, became second nature. With the Solent atlas I also learned the subtleties of tidal currents. For example, the streams ran fastest down the deeper southern side of the Solent. So when sailing in the same direction as the current, that was the route to take, as if hitching a ride on the mighty flow. But if I needed to sail against the current – and this was something to avoid whenever possible – the shallower northern side was best. During neaps, the strength of currents everywhere fell by almost half, compared to springs, making all the difference in planning a journey. Entering rivers, which have their own currents, could also depend on the tide. With the tide rising,

I could float up rivers almost without effort, but on a falling tide the outward currents could be fierce, making the last stretch before tying up for the night an unexpected hurdle. For the first time in my life I began to keep regular checks on the stages of the moon.

This new knowledge was standard to sailors, but to me felt like treasure, and in a way it was: my invitation to the magical, endless dance of the planets, stars and sea.

Great solo circumnavigators like the nineteenth-century Bostonian Joshua Slocum and Frenchman Bernard Moitessier a century later were able to go for long periods without land or human contact save brief conversations with the crews of passing ships. This did not just mean that they could put up with the absence of land and people; rather, they ceased viewing the sea as something that lay between two comforts, or between real life, in the way, say, that passengers of a ferry or liner would. To them, and particularly to Moitessier, the sea took on such importance that at times it was hard to distinguish when they were really at home – was it while in port or while alone on the high seas? In other words, they had been liberated from land.

For both Slocum and Moitessier, this closeness to the sea was possible only because of their closeness to their boats. Obviously, it is the boat that allows man on to the sea in the first place and anything that floats will do the basic job. But Slocum's *Spray* and Moitessier's *Joshua* went a stage further, being such fine ocean-crossing vessels that they became almost human themselves, bonding not only with their captains but with the sea itself. Slocum on several occasions marvelled at the way *Spray* kept her course when rigged to self-steer as he slept, while both he and Moitessier constantly referred to their yachts as living creatures, rather than mere technical aids. For Moitessier, *Joshua* was an equal partner in a joint adventure. 'Don't look beyond *Joshua*, my little red and white planet made of space, pure air, stars, clouds and freedom in its deepest, most natural sense,' he said. 'Live only with the sea and my boat, for the sea and for my boat.'

The better I understood not only *Aquila-Gilliatt* but also the sea, the clearer these notions became and the more I longed to cut my ties to land. I didn't need a yacht, for this was a question of state of mind – a dinghy would do. The key, I was sure, was in the transition from sailing as a hobby to sailing as a journey, where the boat was not a toy but an equal: together you triumphed, together you weathered difficulties, together you built a relationship with the sea. Of this I'd had an inkling all along, but the time had come to make that shift for real.

That meant, despite the cold, keeping on with spending nights out on the water – and as many as I could stand. Between a day sail and spending even one night on board there is a fundamental difference. After twenty-four hours on a dinghy, you get used to having to crouch under the tent, constantly towelling off wet surfaces, nursing the gas cooker, squeezing with sleeping bag into that narrow sleeping space, and watching your balance during everything from peeing over the side to climbing on the bow to change sails. These living arrangements become normal. So one night is already something, but staying even longer, two or three days, say, opens yet another experience. Amazingly, I found that the longer I stayed on *Aquila*, the *less* cramped I felt. This was not just a question of becoming accustomed, rather that I stopped seeing the gunwales as the limits of my home. The boat was the centre, yes, but home extended far across the water all around – as far, in fact, as I could possibly sail. To understand that was to understand the freedom of journeying on the sea.

The short days meant that I was usually swinging on the anchor line or tied to a buoy by 5 p.m. and alone in a cold dark for the next fifteen hours. Sometimes I arrived in the rain with water in the bottom of the boat, my oilskins glistening, my hands and feet cold. Neither was my old sleeping bag so great. But *Aquila* never let me down and with a little improvisation a reasonably comfortable night could always be had. In addition to my little gas cooker, I bought a gas lamp which gave an intense, warming light to burn off the gloom of those long evenings and allow me to read and write. I slept in my clothes with the oilskins draped over the top of the sleeping bag to keep out the wind, and when that was still not enough I wore the oilskins too. Because they were of the non-breathable kind, they insulated heat and stopped wind so well that, when added to my otherwise threadbare sleeping bag, I could have slept on a mountain.

On a few occasions in January and February I gave in and spent nights on land. Once, I sailed to Cowes, tacked up the river past the *Red Osprey* ferry, a push-me-pull-you contraption with a bow at each end, past dredging ships and barges, past the chain ferry and the forests of masts in the boatyards, then glided under almost no wind to the pontoons of a sailing school where beds could be had for £10 a night. I'd wanted, as usual, to sleep aboard, but temperatures had been under zero all day – so cold that my breath came out in smoke and the wet boat tent I had folded under the bows froze into slabs. So it was that *Aquila* spent the night tied up at the sailing school, protected by my latest purchase of four rubber fenders, while I slept in a bed. But all night I dreamed I was moving through the sea and I couldn't wait to get back on board. People hurrying past the pontoon in the drizzle and chill the next morning did double-takes when they noticed me hunched over the stove in my oilskins brewing tea. Mad, no doubt they thought, but nothing could have dragged me away.

Still reading and re-reading the sailing manuals, all my earliest lessons were repeated in the cauldron of Force 5s and 6s. To reef when alone in choppy seas, with the boat rocking and the wind whipping anything loose into a frenzy, was dicey. You had first to 'heave-to', the technique of turning the foresail and the rudder against each other to stall the boat, then, ignoring the sea surging up to the gunwale edges, crawl by the mast to take down the sail and haul in the reefs. This was about like trying to tie your shoelaces while balanced on a fairground bumper car, but in time I came to trust the heave-to position and often put *Aquila* into this in order not to reef but simply to eat lunch, or look at the chart. Likewise, I practised and re-practised tacking, or beating to windward; it was a matter of learning how far *Aquila* could heel without going over and steering through the waves. Sometimes I could thread the gaps, sometimes it was better to meet the wave straight on and sometimes I could run up at a slight angle, then slide down the other side, always mindful not to let the waves break on our beam, a sure way to get swamped or capsize.

The more confident I became, the more I was able to experiment. I might sail against the current or change my sails or reef when I didn't need to, then change them back. I took down the sails and rowed for hours, flying along with the tide or fighting almost to tears against. I sailed for the first time beyond Cowes and over to Portsmouth. I deliberately sought out the shipping lanes into Southampton to understand how to cross the path of the cargo vessels, maybe the biggest hazard of the modern Channel. I bought a waterproof sleeve for my charts, which, rolled up and stuffed behind a bench, were always ready for quick consultation. Then I fitted a compass to the central bench and practised the tricky discipline of steering accurately to a bearing from one buoy marked on the chart to another.

Aquila also underwent some improvements. Although it hadn't seemed that way at the time, I had really bought her in a most basic state. For her to carry me in all weathers on trips around the Solent, let alone to sail to France, a good bit more change was needed. Luckily I'd found Tony Smee, a Wayfarer sailor himself who had just started his own business looking after dinghies. I think I was his first customer. He may have been surprised when I explained what I wanted, but Tony, as if sent by the sea, understood from the start. He was one of the few people I trusted to tell that I planned to cross the Channel.

In this second refit, Tony strengthened every fitting, from the rudder to the mast foot to the shrouds (cables holding the mast in place). Screws were replaced with nuts and bolts, slabs of wood were placed between the fibreglass and bolts, old ropes were replaced, and the scrapes and chips in the hull, centreboard and rudder were filled and smoothed out. Perhaps the biggest single advance was that from now on I no longer had to watch helplessly as *Aquila* filled with water in rough conditions. In the past, I'd had a hand-held pump and a bucket, but to use them required both hands and that meant stopping, something difficult in the very conditions when the

167

most water came aboard. By the time I got to shelter where I could tie up and bail in safety, there might easily be ten to twenty buckets of water sloshing around the floorboards, a dangerous amount of weight to have shifting from one side of the boat to the other when tacking. Now, though, I had 'self-bailers', two valves cut into the centre of the hull that as long as the boat was moving would suck out any water inside. As a back-up, I also had a pump screwed on under one of the benches with a hose going over the side, a contraption that was easy to use one-handed. The other new arrow in my quiver was a change to the rigging so that from now I could have both the large foresail, the genoa, and the small jib attached and ready to use. Before, changing from the genoa to the jib, or vice versa, had again been possible only when stationary, or when hove-to in calm conditions – in other words, impossible when I really needed it. Now, though, I could go out with the genoa furled and the jib up, or the genoa opened and the jib lashed to the foredeck, the change-over taking a matter of minutes. *Aquila* was becoming a true sea boat.

While at sea, never did I feel lonely, for I was never alone: I had *Aquila*, the jungle of marsh birds, the visits by curious swans, and the constant dressing and undressing of the tide. I did, though, often feel a stranger, allowed on to the sea as an exception. It did not matter that I knew every corner of the Solent well from the summer, because in winter those mud dunes of Newtown or the bleak shingle stretches at Hurst were another world. Gone were the crowded, cosy anchorages and mooring spots of the tourist season. Gone were the sounds of laughter in the evenings, the smell of barbecues, the drone of small outboard motors and the dips of oars. The land was grey now, the water dark, the moorings always free. Entering these places, I couldn't help feeling as if *Aquila* and I were creating a disturbance. And only gradually did this sensation change, as if, little by little, we were winning the trust of the sea. The breakthrough, the moment when I no longer felt like having to apologize to the sea, when I knew that *Aquila* and I had been accepted at last, came unexpectedly one night.

The plan had been to make the short hop from Lymington to Hurst Castle bay late in the afternoon, then spend the night at anchor, ready for sailing the following day. I was late, though, in launching, very late, and the sun had set by the time I was under way. The wind, which had been forecast as light, had whipped up to Force 5 or 6. However, I could not face dismantling the boat, giving up and finding a place to sleep in town, and so, nervously, I reached out of Lymington river and began tacking up to Hurst in the dusk. I had the tide with me but the wind against, and the sea was moderately rough. Perhaps just to cheat myself, I'd hoped against all logic that I might make the two miles before the very last light had gone, but even by the time I was out of the river and into the Solent the dark sky and sea had intertwined. A long forty-five minutes or so ensued, forty-five minutes of exhilaration as I cut through a boisterous sea I couldn't see, before I reached the shingle spit outside Hurst Castle bay.

The entrance to the bay is narrow, tucked to the side and unlit. Even close up I could see nothing but the low black bulk of the shingle, the mud banks and terra firma merging into one. There was not a single boat in view and in the bay, which is a nature reserve, not a sign of human life. Reaching along very close to the Solent side of the shingle spit, I strained my eyes for the entrance, concentrating so hard that it was

169

only in an oblique way that I realized I was afraid. Voices urged me to give in and sail back to the safety of Lymington, but those two more miles in the dark and in this wind would quite possibly be more dangerous yet. I kept searching. Distances were impossible to judge and in the same second I might think I was safely off the land, then realize that waves were breaking just metres ahead. I could be wrecked. The thought had never seemed so obvious yet so surreal. I could be wrecked at night. *Aquila* could be lost. And I?

When I did find the entrance, visible because it was a slightly lighter shade of black than the land on each side, I felt not triumph but a great happiness. As I let out the anchor and began to bunker down for the night, I knew this was not the kind of thing one was meant to do in a dinghy. Sailing alone at night in such conditions would be described as irresponsible or unseamanlike in all the learning manuals. But I'd done it, I'd arrived, and in my heart I truly didn't feel I'd done wrong. With our arrival in Hurst Castle bay, *Aquila-Gilliatt* and I had come home.

Often I passed shellfish dredgers in the Solent, or trawlers on their way further out to sea, but for all the time I'd spent on the water and in harbours along the Channel, I'd never been on a fishing boat. Not many people had. Fishermen kept an almost tribal distance from landlubbers. When in harbour, their boats might be in the thick of the tourists and seaside day-trippers, yet they took no notice. When passing other boats at sea, they seldom waved the way yacht sailors almost always did. And I understood why: theirs was a serious business. There had been times, when it was rough or especially cold and I was out sailing alone, when they did wave to me, a kind of salute maybe. Once, a fishing boat, the usual scarred iron hulk crewed by equally rough-looking men, came alongside as I tried to row *Aquila* against the tide into Lymington harbour. 'Do you want us to give you a tow in?' the man whom I took for the captain asked. Rowing against the current was a real fight, but because it was a real fight and a fight I'd been at already for half an hour, I turned the offer down. I wanted to beat this thing on my own. The fisherman beamed and to encourage me flexed his long right arm in Popeye fashion. I laughed so hard that I lost my rhythm and a good twenty metres of ground gained to boot. That iron man congratulating me on my so-called toughness. What a joke!

Such contacts with fishermen were warm but rare, and as most other people I could only look on these huntsmen of the sea and wonder. So when I received an invitation to spend a few days on a French trawler out of the port of Granville, I did not hesitate. It would mean leaving *Aquila* behind for a while, but it was also a chance to learn from the people who more than any others had made the Channel their home.

Arriving in Cherbourg aboard yet another ferry, I met the organizer of my trip, a magnificent woman named Béatrice Harmel, who represented fishermen of lower Normandy from an office in the city's docks. Her full title was Secrétaire Générale, Comité Régional des Pêches Maritimes et des Elevages Marins de Basse-Normandie, and it was Madame Harmel who battled the likes of Dougal Lane in Guernsey over fishing rights around the Channel Islands. With her lampshade haircut, green eyes and big voice full of mirth, she must have been a formidable opponent. When I asked about the complaints from Channel Islands fishermen over the behaviour of French boats, she exhaled a mushroom cloud of Gauloise, put down her coffee cup and chortled. 'It's not a dispute about fish. It's to do with sovereignty. Guernsey feels insecure and it needs to throw its weight around,' she said. 'They have problems, because they're not part of the EU and because they're being looked at by London, with their tax haven and bank accounts from who knows where. They don't give a damn about fishing in Guernsey. They push the fishermen aside.' Even when I asked about the well-documented case in which a French trawler allegedly destroyed the fishing gear of a Guernseyman, she was undeterred: 'That [Guernsey] fisherman, he wants war. He's capable of anything – even of taking stuff from his own people to make it look like it was us.' Then, in her winning style, she dismissed the case in another cloud of smoke and said, 'Ah, well, there are always *moutons noirs*.'

Madame Harmel had good news. The boat she'd been trying to arrange would be leaving from Granville for four days of trawling late on Sunday evening, giving me two days to play with beforehand. So, leaving Granville to my north, I drove down, from curiosity, to the bay of Mont-St-Michel, where the abbey rose like a spectre from the mud flats. Just a little further on, I found myself in the heart of the bay's shellfish industry. Here, amphibious boats with flat-bottomed hulls and lorry wheels harvested hidden crops of shellfish out at low tide, restaurants all specialized in *fruits de mer* and everywhere the tang of oysters filled the air. At a sleepy place called Vivier-sur-Mer, I stopped at a roadside hut selling *moules-frites* at thirty francs and fish soup. A dusty wind blew off the bay and across the road the corrugated-iron roof of an oyster and mussel depot glinted in the sun. Thierry, an oyster-monger, showed me the best way to open the oyster, gave me the practice victim to eat, then sold me the knife. A

smart man. He also told me something about oyster culti-
vation.

There'd been a time when oysters were thought of as
inexhaustible in the bay of Mont-St-Michel, but they were
not, for the oyster is a surprisingly fragile creature and over
the years has fallen victim to a variety of man-made and natural
ills. The latest affliction was the invasion of the bay by an
American mollusc called the slipper limpet, or *Crepidula fornicata*, that had already spread over other areas of northern Europe,
but had spared France until more recently. Now, unopposed,
this mollusc, with its brownish, strawberry-sized shell, was
infesting the seabed, sucking up food needed by oysters and in
some places quite literally blanking out all other life. No one
was quite sure how the invader had arrived, but the first sightings
had been after the Second World War, precisely around those
beaches where the great D-Day landings took place. So
although it was possible that other slipper limpets had been
accidentally introduced alongside imported shellfish, the suspicion among scientists and locals was that the *Crepidula fornicata*
had made its own Normandy invasion. Half a century on, the
molluscs were out of control. Their astonishing rate of repro-
duction, true to their name, seemed almost perverse and even
the brightest minds could not think what to do.

'Surely you could eat them, Thierry,' I said. 'You eat snails.
We eat whelks. That would be the best revenge.'

'I don't think so,' he said, smiling. 'People have tried, but
it's hard to persuade the public. They even tried to give it a
better name, because *Crepidula fornicata* . . . well! They changed
it to "*berlingot de mer*". "*Berlingot*" is a bonbon from Nantes,
but the *Crepidula* is no *bonbon*, I tell you.'

★

Le Lagon motored out of Granville harbour with her crew of four just before midnight. The harbour beacons fell away, the dark sea opened and I felt the thrill of a new adventure. There is probably no profession about which landsmen are more sentimental than fishing. We are charmed by the boats, which conform so well to picture-book boats; by the men in their oilskins; and by the idea that there are still people whose jobs involve more than sitting at desks or driving cars. Fishermen, it seems, live an eternal coffee commercial, a life of camaraderie, early starts and simple but richly deserved rewards. I knew better – of course, I knew better – but how could I entirely expunge years of delusion? As *Le Lagon* chugged briskly out of the Granville harbour walls into the night, I felt a rush of excitement and romance.

Five hours later, *Le Lagon* was rolling in a heavy swell and I was being sick over the rail. Waves broke first on one side of the stern, then the other, flushing the steel deck in a rush of chilly water and ribbons of weed. A few stars shone over the sea. The skipper, Philippe, was still up in the wheelhouse. Down on the working deck with me were the three other crew: Philippe's sons, Fabrice and Emile, and another young lad also called Fabrice. They were putting out the net, a green plastic mesh weighed down by rolls of solid rubber wheels and two giant metal plates. Dressed head to toe in yellow oilskins with hoods the size of monks' cowls, they struggled to balance as they wrestled the net out of the boat and over the stern to sink beneath the black sea. Helpless, I held on to the side and retched. When nothing more came out, I kept retching. Sweat covered my forehead. It was 5 a.m.

The three went back into the galley and smoked in silence in front of a small TV that picked up the main French channels. I tried to join them, but a few seconds later ran out on to the deck and was sick again. By the time I returned, the three had disappeared down a hatch and into their bunks, which were in the hold, below the water line. I followed, squeezing down the ladder into the pitch black and the ripe smell of sweat and wet clothes. My bunk was closed in except for a central aperture, like a tissue-box laid on its side. I hadn't the strength even to feel claustrophobic.

Four hours later, an alarm sounded, a loud electronic blurp – the signal from Philippe in the wheelhouse to get up and take in the net. Up went the three lads, one of them lighting a cigarette as he climbed the ladder. I followed, feeling as if a giant syringe had drained my body. Outside, the scene of the night before was transformed. The black space of the sea and sky was now blue and white. Some way off, quite hazy, was land – one of the Channel Islands. Up came the net on the end of two steel cables and suddenly the deck was a carpet of dying fish. Rays gasped for air, faces human and grotesque, like deflated joke balloons. Dogfish thrashed against each other until their faces became puppy-like and soft. A strange red creature with fins the shape of Spanish fans took his end calmly, bulbous eyes staring without understanding at my booted feet. A crowd of seagulls, the chorus to this tragedy, gathered noisily overhead. The fishermen were content. The rays and a few squid would bring a good price. Back down went the net and the seagulls dispersed.

Unable to take the stench of diesel and fish, I braced myself against the stern and was sick once more. I despaired – there were still three days to go – but seasickness disappears as quickly as it comes and later that day I suddenly felt whole. Emile noticed at once. 'You're OK now.' And I was.

175

At last I was able to climb up into the wheelhouse to see Philippe. Dressed casually and wearing glasses, he could have been a shop assistant, not a boat captain, but then Philippe never had to deal with the nets or the fish, and so he dressed as he liked. Arrayed in a circle around his central chair was a bank of electronic equipment, a far cry from the brutal business that went on below.

A computer terminal displayed a chart of the Channel Islands. The chart system was connected to the Global Positioning System device, so our progress was plotted continuously on the screen, a little triangle marking the position of *Le Lagon*. We were just north of Sark, close to the disputed fishing grounds that Dougal Lane had pointed out to me on his own chart. The computer program also contained charts of every sea in the world. I could drag the mouse across the Atlantic, find details of an anchorage in Hudson Bay, then slide my way back to the Channel Islands, all in a few seconds. If I clicked anywhere on the chart, the computer would say when we'd arrive. 'What about the paper charts and chart tables and all that?' I asked. '*Oh, ça c'est fini maintenant,*' Philippe said. A radar screen tracked every boat in our area and a 'fish-finder' picked up the presence of shoals of fish. Sonar also showed the shape of the seabed, allowing Philippe to avoid any dangerous humps that could snag the net. As for steering, the computer handled that too; the traditional wooden wheel in the forward position had not yet been touched. In the corner glowed Philippe's own television. 'When I started twenty-six years ago there was none of this. The boats were smaller and so were the nets, but then there were more fish,' Philippe said. Now the race was in the other direction.

For the rest of the day and the night and the next day and

next night the rhythm never changed. Roughly four hours of trawling up and down a carefully chosen bit of seabed, then the nets came up, the fish were packed into ice-filled crates and the nets went back down. When the nets were down the crew could sleep or eat, but never for more than those few hours, while Philippe almost never slept at all. Food was put through the hatch to his wheelhouse as if to a prisoner in solitary confinement. When they were not sleeping or working, the men sat in the galley, smoked and watched TV. There was little conversation. They never got out of their clothes, awake or asleep, and almost never washed. Sleep in that dank underwater chamber, with just a thin wooden wall separating one from the thud of the engine, was easy only because of the exhaustion. And if anything went wrong and required extra work, sleep lost out, not the putting down or lifting up of nets. During one trawl, a net snagged and tore. It would take all three lads, working as fast as they could, ten hours to repair. This they did instead of sleeping, sewing new sections of reserve netting to what was left of the old, as *Le Lagon* pitched and rolled her way through the disputed seas. It was the life of frontline defenders in war, or of astronauts in restless orbits of the Earth, a new night and a new day every forty-five minutes.

On the second night we fished the Sark Box. This was one of the most contested areas, a rich fishing ground west of Jersey and south of Guernsey, where Guernsey since 1994 had been trying, with little success, to exclude French boats. I went up to see Philippe. After the damp, the fish scales, the cigarette butts and the noise below, his post was a welcome haven. Besides, he always had a welcoming smile, however tired he was, while the lads below were cold. They weren't hostile, just too busy and too tough to be anything but cold, even among themselves.

'There's been a patrol boat watching, so we're being careful to stay on the right side of the border,' Philippe said, his face lit up by display panels and the tireless television, where, unwatched, a late-night actress moaned with pleasure.

I asked about the fishing dispute. 'It's practically war,' Philippe said. *Le Lagon* had been part of a fleet that recently 'invaded' Guernsey's harbour to support the detained skipper of a French trawler, *La Confiance*, while Philippe himself had been arrested a few years back. For what he said was an accidental crossing of the territorial line just west of Guernsey, he and another trawler captain were imprisoned, fined and had their nets and fish confiscated. 'We'd been taking up the nets close to the line and the current simply pushed us over,' he said. 'All night we'd been fishing on the correct side. We could even prove that by showing the tracks recorded on the screen there, but they wouldn't take this into account. It can be really serious, arrest and being fined.' The skipper of *La Confiance* had almost been ruined, he said. 'He had to go to the bank and reschedule his loans and so on. Luckily the local committee helped him.'

Emile then came up to take command and Philippe went down below with me for one of his first rests of the voyage.

When I woke later that night I couldn't find my watch and realized that I was unable to guess the time. Even at midday not a thread of light penetrated the hold, so it could be morning for all I knew. It didn't matter. By now my land rhythm had been broken and that of the sea was taking over. Pulling on my boots and coat, I squeezed up through the hatch and out of the galley on to the deck. It was night. The nets were down – I could see the steel cables trailing into the black sea – and there was no one about, just the diesel engine and the TV, which were such constants I'd come to think of them as crew members. Not wanting to go back to my bunk, I sat in the galley and read.

A little later, Emile, who'd swapped back with Philippe while I slept, emerged from below. For the first time he greeted me with a broad smile. '*Ça va là? Tu dors pas?*' He made instant coffee, opened what must have been his second or third pack of cigarettes of the voyage and sat opposite. Suddenly we were talking.

Fishing was Emile's destiny. Not only his father fished, but his grandfather had been a trawlerman and his great-grandfather one of those sailors who flourished on both sides of the Channel making nine-month expeditions to New-foundland for cod. Emile had gone to sea at fifteen and now his father was preparing him as a skipper, while his younger brother, Fabrice, would be more the mechanic. The wages for young fishermen in Granville, a well-off port, averaged about 15,000 French francs, or £1,500, a month before tax. Emile made 21,000 FF, but then he worked at least a seventy-five-hour week, had no holidays and rarely more than a day off in a week. Emile had no complaints. He'd been born into this life. The TV flickered overhead, seemingly more incongruous all the time – tampon ads, a cowboy film, a game show – but when the news came on, we both looked up. France was on strike again. Recently there'd been the students and now it was the turn of the pharmacy workers. Footage from the previous day showed them in their white coats marching through Paris. Emile looked on in disbelief, verging on pity. 'Do you believe that?'

On the fourth day, we tied up in Granville and climbed a long, thin iron ladder to the top of the harbour wall. A crane lifted the fish from the hold – eighty-three ice-filled crates in all, fetching 45,000 FF at the auction on the quay. 'Not bad,' said Philippe, phlegmatic as ever. We said our goodbyes. The weather forecast was rough for the next day. 'Will you be going out?' I asked Emile, wishing at once that I hadn't. 'Of course,' he replied with a forgiving smile.

I paused on the road up the Normandy coast to Le Havre and my ferry home. This was haunted territory. D-Day landing museums, monuments and even signposted routes – '*objectif: un port*', '*la percée*', '*l'encerclement*' – allowed tourists to choose their battle, but at the same time barely a crater or other real mark of violence had been left. The war was advertised but invisible, left to the ghosts in the bocage and the cemeteries that stretched like petrified forests, lonely as the beaches where the soldiers fell. Remnants of a Mulberry harbour, the prefabricated breakwaters brought in by the Allies, loomed from the water off Arromanches beach. Here, in a strange way there was a living link to the past: the most likely way the *Crepidula fornicata* first invaded France would have been on the sides of these Mulberry harbours, not the naval boats themselves. First, these giant structures had been assembled in the *Crepidula*-rich habitats of southern England, giving the limpets plenty of time to attach themselves. Second, the Mulberry harbours were never taken away after the war, meaning that the limpets then had all the conditions to start their conquest.

Arromanches was deserted except for a few sand sailors wheeling over the endless beach. The chunks of Mulberry harbour made it just possible to trace the line of the former breakwater. Only a conjuror, though, could summon back the rest of the scene – the jetties attached to the Mulberry walls, the thousands upon thousands of armed men, the big ships and landing craft, the smoke, lorries and the steady thump of artillery. Again, this was a place of D-Day's ghosts, but if those theories about the *Crepidula* coming in with the Allies were correct, then there was one wraith that perhaps I could resurrect.

I parked the car, walked barefoot for what seemed for ever across hard, rippled sand and, wearing a cheap pair of goggles, entered the opaque sea. At once I made for the nearest section of Mulberry harbour, a great concrete hulk where the edges swirled with currents and breaking waves. Having seen some of the *Crepidula* in the bay of Mont-St-Michel, I knew what to look for: the little brown shells stuck to each other in families of a dozen or so, forming a cluster that looked like an armoured fist. So convinced was I by my mission that I half expected to find these fists clinging to the sides of the Mulberrys like grapes. But although mussels blackened the concrete, there was not a sign of the slipper limpet. I tried diving, but the goggles were useless.

On the point of giving up, I noticed a small green wooden fishing boat with one old man aboard heading towards the beach. He and I were the only people in the water as far as the eye could see and on impulse I waved my arms and shouted. To my surprise the fisherman came over – maybe he thought I was drowning – and let me hang to the gunwales of his craft while I explained. He looked mystified and said he'd never heard of the *Crepidula*.

I swam back, despondent. If there were no slipper limpets on the beach they supposedly started at, then these theories looked flimsy and most likely the problem started with something as prosaic as an accidental introduction during the importation of some other seafood. Up on the beach, two men carrying shrimp nets and wicker baskets passed me on their way to the water. I hesitated, but on an off chance turned after them and asked again about the *Crepidula*. Again, looks of bewilderment. I walked away.

Suddenly a shout. '*Eh oh!* What did you call them? *Crepidula?*'

Heart pounding, I ran to the shrimpers. 'Do you mean these?' There, just where the incoming tide licked the beach, lay one of those peculiar fists of shells. Somehow I'd missed them. 'They grow *that* high out in the deeper water,' the shrimper said, extending his arms with an expression between awe and horror. I looked carefully and found another bunch washed up, then another and another. Here, quite possibly, were direct descendants of the D-Day invaders, simple sea creatures far from home but brilliantly adaptable, hated yet relentlessly successful. I picked up a bunch and at once the fist, although unattached to any arm, began to wriggle. I dropped it on to the sand, my revulsion mixed with something unexpected: the first stirrings of admiration.

On the night ferry back to Portsmouth, I waited until we were under way and took a turn of the deck. There was nothing to see in the dark other than a glimpse of white wake. Most passengers were asleep, except for some at the bar, which would soon close. But when I looked out, the Channel teemed with stories. I thought of the men of *Le Lagon*, those astronauts of the sea. I thought of the boat traps of the Channel Islands to my south-west. I thought of the silent, frightful march of the *Crepidula* under the calm waters of Mont-St-Michel. I thought of Jean-Luc and André, the shipyard workers I'd met in Le Havre before boarding the ferry. The vessel they were building, a tanker called *Stolt Perseverance*, had been the last order their yard would ever have. She lay now on her slipway, gleaming, fattened, oblivious to the despair of the men who created her. In a few days, she would be launched, and the shipyard, the last in Le Havre, would shut down and 2,000 jobs would disappear.

Water is soft, but the sea is a hard place, and in the end it is always water, not rock or iron, that lasts longest. This was true even in the Channel, that apparently tame old sea we were crossing tonight with barely a thought. *Especially* in the Channel. But who on this ferry would know? I myself was only just beginning to find out.

5

S pring makes no grand entrance at sea. There are no flowers and buds to wipe winter away and neither the waves nor the winds seem to pay any attention at all. But in one respect I noticed the change in season more than at any time in my life: there was light and every day a little more. I wanted nothing else. Released from the dark, *Aquila* and I went further all the time. Where once a trip of five miles seemed enough, I gave no thought now to passages of ten to fifteen miles, from Lymington to Southampton water, say, or from Keyhaven to Cowes, then back to Beaulieu. I was creeping up on the distance of the Dover Straits and I knew I could do better.

This new rhythm and the knowledge that the day of my crossing to France was approaching turned my mind to old Frank Lawrence's admonition about navigation. I hadn't yet thought much about where I would cross, but wherever it was I would be far from land. What about the currents over such a long distance – surely I'd be pushed far off course? And how would I find my harbour on the other side? I'd be arriving in another country on shores I'd never seen from the sea, a far cry from my homecomings in the familiar waters of the Solent. Then there were all those ships mid-Channel, hundreds passing between Dover and Calais every day. From what I'd seen outside Southampton, they moved very fast, from picture-book ships safely on the horizon to surging steel hulks the size of apartment blocks ten or fifteen minutes later. 'Be careful of large ships,' my *Beginner's Guide* said. 'They are almost always going much faster than they seem to be.' I needed training and so, that March, in the film-set emptiness of London's Docklands, I began attending a course on navigation.

Here I got many answers: how to plot a course that takes into account the effects of current; how to determine a position by taking bearings off landmarks, by sounding depths or by calculating course and distance travelled; how to determine tide levels at different times at any place; the regulations for safe crossing of shipping lanes; the intricacies of buoyage and navigational markings; even weather forecasting. As for the practical side of the course – chart reading, knots, anchors and sailing techniques – I'd been dealing with this in my own amateur way for months. Even the more scientific material made sense when I thought of *Aquila* and, before long, I had become the keenest manipulator of dividers and ruler, the most fanatical checker of calculations, the king of pencil sharpeners, an addict of charts. I was enthralled. With five small implements – brass dividers, a 2HB pencil, a rubber and a compass and protractor – and a little knowledge, I finally had the keys to the chart and, with the chart, to navigating the sea.

In the beginning, my idea of sailing had been to point *Aquila-Gilliatt* out of Keyhaven, aim for an easily visible point and hope to arrive. Later, when I'd understood the tides, I'd time my passage for favourable currents, or take measures to compensate for the wrong drift. Now I could make each outing a miniature voyage, with courses that took into account the tides plotted from the chart, estimated times of arrival, fallback plans in case of adverse conditions and careful checks for potential hazards or unexpected eddies of current I might meet on the way. A year before I'd been about as poorly

188

prepared as those men who first navigated the Channel in log and skin boats, but now I was catching up. In months, I'd advanced through several eras of sailing.

In April I readied *Aquila* for our biggest voyage to date, setting eastward from Lymington on a Friday lunchtime. A generous northerly Force 3 and the tide in my favour ate the coastline: the Beaulieu river entrance – six miles gone; crossing over to Cowes harbour – nine or ten miles gone; on around the corner of Wight, passing Queen Victoria's holiday retreat, Osborne House, and down to Wootton Creek – fourteen miles gone. That was originally as far as I'd planned to go, but the steady march of passing miles and harbours was infectious. I kept going. Now sailing on a broad reach, I cleated down the main and jib controls, kept the tiller straight with a length of bungee cord and sat back to whistle. The spires of Ryde shot up to the south – almost sixteen miles. Here, sand shallows bulge out for more than a mile, discolouring the water and trapping the unwary, or disrespectful. At that very moment a white motor launch sat helplessly aground, her abject crew in conference at the stern, although with the tide rising, they'd soon be lifted off and away; they had nothing to fear. In the shipping lane, about a mile out, container ships and tankers in red and blue and yellow moved ponderously towards Southampton, like cattle coming into the barn. The wind was picking up, but there were still three hours of daylight left. I steered into deeper water, towards the shipping lane, my destination Bembridge, the last good harbour on the east side of the Isle of Wight.

Standing guard over the shipping lane were two extraordinary objects: Horse Sand Fort and No Man's Land Fort. They were two of four similar forts built in the 1860s as permanently anchored, unsinkable battleships to block the eastern approaches of the Solent against French iron-clads. So out of place were these mutant vessels, their immobility in such contrast to the ships sliding by, that it seemed they had to be something far stranger than merely old forts. Spaceships immediately came to mind or ghastly temples of sacrifice. Finally I decided that they must be the pedestals of a fallen colossus, one for each giant leg. For Bembridge, I only had to turn south-east, but I couldn't resist the forts' eerie, impossible presence in the middle of the sea and so, frightened and attracted, I steered for No Man's Land.

At medium range, the circular bulk of the fort became only more menacing, a scarred and scabby monster in black iron and stone, but when I got really close, this stunted tower suddenly softened. The gunports I'd seen were now windows. Flower baskets hung outside what looked like a suburban bungalow that had been attached on top. A motorboat hung on a crane high above the waves. Inside that bungalow, a light shone. Only later did I discover that I'd seen the tip of an iceberg. No Man's Land Fort was the private plaything of an English-born tax exile, an art-filled pleasure dome hiding a vast wine cellar, swimming pool, restaurant, disco, helicopter pad and space for hundreds of guests, including the master bedroom with a rotating bed in the small lighthouse.

On the leeward side of the fort I crossed a patch of mirror-smooth water before re-entering the regular chop and reaching south to Bembridge. The wind was up to Force 5 now and the red whistling buoy I passed keened like a mother bereaved. Ahead of me, the crackle of surf and the smaller fort of St Helen's: the entrance to Bembridge harbour —

twenty-one miles. Tide rising, sun falling, clouds gathering. I had *Aquila* docked and the boat tent on just as the first rains came.

The members of the local sailing club were filled with concern Saturday morning when I climbed up on to the pontoon. The wind had swung to the north-east and reached Force 7 during the night, knocking small waves against the pontoon and shaking *Aquila* like a sapling. The only real sleep I got was at low tide, when the water went right out and for a few hours *Aquila* settled on solid ground. By morning, temperatures were in the low single digits and the rain still hadn't paused. The water in the harbour was grey. I'd planned to sail to Chichester, seven miles to the north-east, but there would be heavy cold seas out there today and the wind was head-on. For the first time on any of my trips, I was stuck in harbour. For how long? At least a day and a night. The next day's weather was still uncertain. Oddly, though, I liked the uncertainty, for relying on the sea and the wind was what I'd wanted all along and now I was in rhythm with the elements. In the sailing club, a crusty gent, evidently a man of importance, had turned his nose up at my salt-caked clothes and uncombed hair, then recommended in as patronizing a voice as possible that later I 'come in and at least get some decent food'. But I had already decided: however cold and wet, my enforced stay in Bembridge would be on *Aquila*. No B&B, no restaurants; *Aquila-Gilliatt* was home.

In the afternoon I stopped at the Bembridge Shipwreck Museum. Strange, I thought, how the bottles, binnacles, fragments of ships' names and cannonballs that appear in these places always have the same look. Whether restored to gleaming brass or left encrusted and corroded as found on the seabed, shipwreck artefacts seem uniformly forlorn. They also seem ageless, as if a seventeenth-century galleon and a modern tanker become the same once they touch the seabed. The objects were not always interesting in themselves – a cannon-ball is just a round metal lump – but each was the thread end that must eventually lead to a much greater fabric still hidden under the sea. A window that I guessed came from the bridge of a reasonably modern ship hung on the wall. The frame was of unblemished brass, but the glass, although very strong, had been shattered. Cracks ran through the pane like lines in a thick sheet of ice. What violence there must have been here, right at the bridge, right where the captain and his officers in their gold braid and white caps, with their charts and sextant, with all the power of engineering at their fingertips, stood night and day in command. A little typewritten sheet nearby told the story.

In February 1917, the troopship SS *Mendi, en route* from South Africa to the war in France, was just south of the Isle of Wight a couple of hours before dawn when the fog came down. Military regulations stipulated that no navigational lights were to be used and so *Mendi* sailed on, her officers, no doubt, crowded on the bridge as lookouts, eyes straining. Without warning, the bows of the liner *Darro* appeared from the fog and hit *Mendi* full-on. Twenty minutes later she had vanished, with the loss of 650 men. Nearly all of the dead were Africans of the Nigerian Regiment. Their story, quite typically for the time, remained almost unheard. What a story. These men had boarded at Cape Town and were on their way to the trenches in France, only to be swallowed first by the restless, unforgiving Channel. Now, this cracked bridge window, hung on a wall in Bembridge, was their tombstone.

Walking back to the harbour, I paused at the sight of *Aquila*. Her white, double-chine hull had never looked so delicately balanced, or her green tent so snug against the elements. Just the manner in which she lay at dock, swinging slightly this way and that in the agitated water, had the air of a serious boat, a boat that was confident in the water, a handsome but very tough vessel. I caught my breath. I'd been slightly dreading the moment of crawling back in under the tent to restart the fight against cold and damp, but not any longer. I looked at *Aquila* and felt a flood of pride. Almost alone among the hibernating yachts of Bembridge, that little ship would soon be going back to sea.

Late that evening the wind veered south and the sun appeared for the first time in twenty-four hours. Temperatures would hit zero overnight, but I no longer cared, for the storm had broken and the next day would be perfect for the long haul home. I dropped into the sailing club to thank the people there for allowing me to use their pontoon. The man of importance was gone and the rest were decidedly good sorts. Someone offered me a drink, another invited me to come in for coffee on his yacht, and the young waitress blushed and said she'd thought I must have been miserable the previous night. In the back of my head was the memory of that débâcle in Keyhaven harbour on my first day in *Aquila*, the embarrassment of knowing that people had watched and guilt at even owning such a boat. Now *Aquila* was again the centre of attention. People had been whiling away the time just by looking down on to the pontoon where she lay. I didn't mind. I felt that pride again and I could turn down all the offers of kindness in the club with an easy heart – *Aquila-Gilliatt* would look after me. Waving goodbye, I cast off and rowed a little way to spend the night at a different pontoon, one in deeper water so that the next day I'd be able to get away at first tide.

In the morning I meant to make straight for Keyhaven to spend that night in the bay of Hurst Castle. However, as soon as I glided out of Bembridge river in bright low sunshine, I could not resist pointing north-east across the open sea for Chichester, seven miles away, just for the sensation of all that water. An hour and a half later I heaved to 100 metres off Chichester, crawled up to the bow to fix a tangle in the furling line for the foresail, drank tea from a Thermos and turned *Aquila* around for Cowes. Carried by the full flood tide, I was soon heading for the familiar confines of the eastern Solent.

Instead of the usual expanse of deserted water, a remarkable landscape presented itself to me on rounding the headland to Cowes. More than a dozen square-rigged ships, some of them of the type I'd seen only in films, were making their way in stately procession out of Southampton. Some glistened in white, others sported piratical rows of gunports and black gunwales. Some had no sails up, their rigging bare as scaffolding, but a few had unfurled the rectangular sails, white as the clouds coming in from the south. Swarming around these giants were the gnats of yachts and motor launches. They criss-crossed in every conceivable direction, all at different speeds and without attention to the laws of right of way at sea, as if the whole yacht fleet of southern England were bent on mutual destruction. Further down the Solent floated a still more incongruous vessel: P&O's monstrous new cruise liner *Aurora*, escorted by her own flotilla of yachts and launches. Beyond them all, like the parent at a riotous teenage party, cruised a Royal Navy warship, low-slung and sober.

Tearing into the middle of this mayhem, *Aquila* kept her westerly course. I would have stayed, but the motorboat people, drivers not sailors, were a danger. The wakes of their boats furrowed the already choppy headland of East Cowes into a grid of confused waves. Already I'd taken two full-strength loads of wake on the bow after vessels the size of trucks shot close past and I didn't fancy putting *Aquila* through anything worse. I kept on west. Three hours later, sped on by winds building to Force 5, I dropped anchor in Hurst Castle bay.

Warmed by my gas lamp, a book in hand and eating my last food stores, I felt rather smug as I settled down for the night. I'd sailed thirty-two miles that day – as far as I'd need to go in crossing the Channel – and never before had I felt such a master of my situation. But the sea, if it hates anything, must hate hubris most, for hubris never goes unpunished.

I first woke about 1 a.m. *Aquila* was swinging badly at anchor. The wind had increased to Force 7, a near gale, and had changed round to the west, meaning I no longer had the protection of the Isle of Wight. The sight outside the back of the boat tent snapped me from drowsiness. The formerly tranquil bay seethed under the light of the moon. White horses, rain and spray flew. *Aquila* pitched, bounced and rocked from side to side on the anchor line. I tried to tell myself that I'd been through this before and could go back to sleep, but gave up minutes later. Spray shot over my face. The wind howled and spat. The tent would probably be torn off before long. In any case, it was the tent that was largely responsible for sending *Aquila* spinning in such violent arcs. I recognized the first signs of seasickness and that really scared me. Alone and seasick, I'd be in trouble.

Suddenly conscious that something serious might happen, either to me or to *Aquila*, I geared for action. First I pulled on my dry suit – that would help me survive whatever happened over the next few hours – then put my boots, oilskins and lifejacket over the top. Next, I stowed away all gear in waterproof bags and stripped off the tent. Our wind resistance was down now, but the rain and spray were coming in, and the waves were still hammering up against the sides. There was worse. Not having expected the change in wind direction, I'd dropped my anchor close by the shore that afternoon to leave *Aquila* swinging safely off the beach. Now that the wind had turned, though, she had veered all the way round to the very shore I'd intended her to avoid. There were waves breaking on that shore, dangerous waves that crashed down on the shingle. As the tide receded and therefore the shoreline crept closer, it looked as if we were soon going to be in those waves. *Aquila* would not get through a battering like that. She'd be pounded to pieces.

Never had I felt so vulnerable and alone on the sea. But I was deeply focused now and with that came a feeling of calm. Somehow I had to regain control of the situation. My first thought was to shorten the anchor line to pull away from the shore. This was difficult. I had to balance up forward fighting the sweats of seasickness and pull the line so hard against the wind and tide that my fingers ached. This was also of limited use, for if I took in too much line, the chances of the anchor holding at all would diminish. Already, the way *Aquila* tossed up and down made me worried that soon either the anchor or the cleat to which the anchor was attached must give. At the best, I could pull myself only a couple of metres further off from the breakers. My next thought was that if I lasted till dawn, then a fisherman might pass. He could tow me. Dawn, though, was several hours away and the waves were getting closer by the minute.

My final thought was to sail away. To sail a Wayfarer during the day in such conditions would be unwise and at night it was ludicrous, but with my options so limited, I thought that nothing could be worse than being smashed on this lee shore. Cold and tired now, I began numbly to prepare to sail. If I could get out of this cursed bay I'd be able to run before the wind under just the foresail to the shelter of Lymington, where the river was well marked and I knew I could find my way in. But I'd hardly started to unfurl the foresail before I abandoned the idea, for the wind was blowing so hard now that I knew I'd be asking for the very worst to happen. I could capsize in the middle of the Solent and be carried away on the current. My sail could be torn, leaving me powerless. I might get swamped by waves I couldn't see. No, I was better off anchored and taking whatever came, when it came.

The clouds burned sulphurous in the moonlight and at one moment terrifying, pitiless eyes seemed to look down at me from the sky. I stared back and slowly, deliberately, made the sign of the cross.

About an hour before low tide, the surf had approached to within a couple of metres of the stern of *Aquila*. Then, at the last moment, a miracle. The steep beach had produced those waves, but at very low water the sea could no longer reach the upper part of the shingle, washing up instead on a much more gentle shelf below. So although the wind was the same and the sea was the same, the waves quite suddenly vanished. I'd been saved by an accident of topography. With at least another two hours before the water rose back to where the waves would build up again, I could wait for dawn and hope that the wind dropped or help came. To stay warm, I climbed – boots, oilskins and all – into my sleeping bag and tucked myself under the bow section of *Aquila*. There was no chance of sleep.

The BBC shipping forecast at 5.35 a.m. confirmed what I'd thought: Force 7 for the Isle of Wight. But shortly after came the first grey light in the east. Like some pagan after an eclipse, I rejoiced. The sun, the sun, the sun. Gulls hidden all night appeared over the beach, as if also encouraged by the dawn. The clouds lit up, bizarre, freakish clouds of every possible shape parading eastward: a lobster the size of Wembley, its delicate arms waving over the sea; elephants; clowns; a witch on a broomstick; a London bus behind a sphinx; a dozen types of fish and eels; a battery of artillery guns, all lined up on one side, and the puffs of their shots all lined up on another. I began to laugh. Nature had terrified me all night, but now had decided to entertain. What style.

The tide was coming well up. No fishermen had appeared and I was glad – the humiliation of being towed into Keyhaven would have been too much. Much better to give sailing another go. Up went the reefed mainsail in a terrific clatter and shaking. In came the anchor, hand over hand, then suddenly free, with my hands full of rope, chain and iron. *Aquila* had probably two seconds now before we blew back on to the shore. I sprang to the tiller, dropped the centreboard a little, took in the mainsail and pushed up on to the windward gunwale. We were away, inches clear of the ground, then into deeper water and then, what bliss, out of the bay and into the Solent. I put a line around my waist, sat out and ran before the wind to Lymington in record time. I was happy. I knew something important: *Aquila-Gilliatt* and I had been tested and we were ready. Next stop France.

The big chart over my desk took on new urgency. Those shaded blues, white, green and mustard yellow would soon transform into real rocks and sand, waves and tides. The purple lines down the middle marking shipping lanes would be busy with the bow waves of great vessels. Some spot along that paper littoral of France would be my landing place. The chart would finally reveal its secrets. But where would I cross and when?

The 'where' inevitably came down to two routes (the same described by Strabo at the time of Christ): one of about eighty miles between Southampton and Cherbourg, the other of twenty-two miles across the Dover Straits. The longer crossing had one advantage in that the central shipping lanes were likely to be much less crowded than the bottleneck of the Straits. However, just eighty miles would probably take *Aquila* fifteen hours, whereas with the effect of at least one ebb and one flood tide sweeping across my path, the actual distance would be considerably more. Even in perfect circumstances, therefore, I'd risk running out of daylight before I closed on the French coast, and if there were any delay at all this would be sure. All sailors prefer to make landfall during daylight – yachts on the long crossing often leave England at night so as to arrive in France after dawn – but alone in *Aquila* this was essential. The short crossing was for me: Dover–Calais or Folkestone–Boulogne.

As for when, there were many precedents. Blériot had flown in July. Swimmers preferred high summer, ideally in August as with Captain Webb's crossing, but sometimes as late as October. Their concern, though, was primarily with water temperature, while for me the main factor was settled winds. I'd need something not more than Force 4 and a direction allowing me to reach across without having to tack, especially in the ten-mile-wide shipping lanes in the centre. But wind was not something that allowed itself to be predicted far in advance. The best forecasters attempted was five days and often that was unreliable. The evacuation of Dunkirk was made possible not so much by the efforts of the Royal Navy and the armada of volunteers, but the enormous luck of calm weather and glassy seas during those last days of May and the start of June 1940. The summer is a fickle beast in the Channel and on many days those 'small ships' would never have been able to leave port. When the time came to set a day for the crossing of the D-Day armada, the best British and American forecasters were unsure until the very last hours whether their predictions had been correct. They'd been asked to pick a date when there would be cloud formations of various types required by bomber and fighter planes, but also a clear moonlit night for gliders, dry ground for the army and light winds and low waves for the navy. A scientific study I found on wave patterns in the Channel said that July had the calmest seas, but in the spring of 1944 the weathermen settled on May or June, then homed in on 5 June and finally postponed after a bout of gales to 6 June. The fiendishly complex weather systems around Britain kept the Allies guessing to the end, but 6 June did indeed prove to be right. June, in that case, would suit me too.

June was the month of the summer solstice and the sun was *Aquila*'s friend, but because of tides the voyage would also be affected by the moon. On this subject I found some useful advice in the Channel Swimming Association handbook. Like the swimmers, I'd be cutting across south-east–north-west tides. Since avoiding tides altogether was impossible, I had to ensure, as the swimming book advised, that my passage was 'timed in order . . . to gain the utmost assistance from the tides'. In other words, as if crossing a river, I'd have to calculate how far upstream to aim in order to finish at the correct part of the French coast. This calculation, simple enough, would be complicated by the international regulation that while in the shipping lanes boats may proceed only at right angles to those lanes, with no compensating angle for slippage allowed. To minimize problems, my best bet was to go, like the swimmers, during neaps, when the tidal currents dropped to about half their maximum strength. Neaps occur about every two weeks, giving two opportunities in June.

Maybe the biggest hazard, at least as much as the wind and waves, was the shipping in the centre of the Channel. Hadn't I read in a yachting magazine that crossing the Atlantic 'would probably be less challenging, and almost invariably less fraught, than a cross-Channel, ship-dodging jaunt to France'? Duncan Taylor had told me the previous summer that 'swimming across the Dover Straits is like having a picnic in the middle of a motorway'. Well, I'd be travelling more than twice the speed of a swimmer, so I'd at least be strolling, maybe jogging. Nevertheless, the same precautions were necessary. A couple of years back there'd been a story about a man who only just survived, after thirty hours drifting around the shipping lanes on a 1.3-metre-wide wooden pallet. I didn't want to share his fate. The Swimming Association handbook, emblazoned with two mermaids holding the organization's crest, gave little comfort. Because 'there are some 500 ships a day making their way up, down or across the Channel', the handbook said, the swimmer had to be protected by his accompanying boat and regular warnings over the VHF radio, courtesy of the coastguard, that 'a Channel swim is in progress . . . A sharp lookout is requested.'

Wondering how sharp those lookouts could be, especially when they'd not been warned about *me*, I accepted the kind invitation of P&O Stena Line's Captain Knowles to accompany him on the bridge of the ferry *Dover* for a return trip across the Straits.

Captain Knowles knew the crossing better than anyone. He did the round trip three times on the days he worked and he worked day-on/day-off for a fortnight, then worked seven nights, then took a week off, before starting all over again. His ship always docked bow first in Calais, stern first in Dover. It was a carefully maintained routine and so far he'd hit no one. Thank God. The *Dover* was 550 feet long, with a height of 130 feet. *Aquila-Gilliatt* was just under sixteen feet, her mast just over twenty-two.

On the *Dover*'s bridge, towering over the bow deck, the atmosphere was that of an operating theatre, windows shaded against bright light, voices kept low. Five other officers were present, one doing paperwork, a couple looking deep into the radar screen, another talking quietly down an oddly old-fashioned-looking telephone, another scanning Dover harbour entrance through binoculars. 'We keep procedures tight. We concentrate so that we can cut out any complacency. No skylarking. As senior master, that's my job,' Captain Knowles said. As soon as we began to depart from Dover all the officers put on their gold-braided caps. 'We make every journey formal,' the captain said. I noticed they called him 'Sir' and that there were a good many 'aye–ayes'. The Dover–Calais job might look like driving a bus, but this lot were definitely sailors.

Once the ferry was under way, the giant front window came to life, but still seemed artificial, as if before I'd been looking at a painting and now a film. Before long we entered the shipping lanes. Someone lent me a pair of binoculars, but there was no need, no need at all. I stared in disbelief. The Dover Straits were a shipping scrum. Vessels came from every direction and in all sizes and colours under the sun – except for any boat even close to the size of *Aquila-Gilliatt*. Nothing could have resembled less the neat purple arrows on the chart. This was what people called the 'Piccadilly of the Sea'. I asked Captain Knowles how he made it across each time. 'Radar,' he said. 'With radar we can see every ship's position and know where they'll be in a few minutes' time.' When the *Dover* was really on a collision course, she would probably just slow down to let the other ship pass.

As casually as possible, almost as if I were joking, I asked whether we were in a good place to cross in a dinghy. 'Just not here, please,' he said. 'This is a tricky little piece of water.' Already, though, I'd ruled out Dover–Calais for my voyage. Much better, I'd head from Folkestone to Boulogne. That was further, but still within my range, and although the east–west shipping traffic would be as great, there'd be only a fraction of the north–south ferries. I was happy, for I'd chosen my path. Besides, Boulogne was the port in which Napoleon dreamed up, then discarded his plans for invading Britain, while Folkestone was home to the English end of the Channel Tunnel. *Aquila-Gilliatt* would be sailing among the Channel ghosts.

The return journey from Calais was enlivened by a family of ferry spotters brought up on to the bridge. They were three – a couple from Manchester and their thirty-year-old daughter – and they were on their annual holiday of taking ferries. 'Every year we come down to Dover for a week and then each day we take the ferry over to France and come back,' said Joyce, the mother. She wore a brown anorak, leather gloves, a brown tartan skirt and a brown scarf. The daughter, Elizabeth, had the same buck teeth, but joyful, shining eyes. Only the father didn't say much. 'We spend some of the day in France,' Joyce continued, 'but then we come back, because it's the ferry we enjoy. Even if we weren't able to get off at the other end, we'd still sail.'

'Yes, every boat's got its own personality,' Elizabeth said. 'We prefer to go on P&O – never SeaFrance. We've made a lot of friends.' I asked if they'd ever been on Eurostar and got hoots of laughter in return. 'Never. We'll only take the ferry,' Elizabeth said. Then, looking at me confidentially, she added, 'We like it when it gets a bit rough.'

'Do you cross often yourself?' asked Joyce.

Now it was my turn to laugh.

My last two nights in Keyhaven were spent on *Aquila*, parked on her trailer in the boatyard. I had odd jobs to do and a few sailing ideas to test. The long-suffering jib had torn and needed replacing; all fittings, especially on the mast and rudder, had to be retightened; a reflector, to signal my presence to ships with radar, needed fixing to the top of the mast; and the jib halyard had to be replaced with a thicker version, giving me better purchase to haul the sail up as tightly as possible.

The boatyard at night had a peculiar atmosphere of its own

– simultaneously deserted and full of life. Strictly speaking, overnight stays were not allowed. During the day there were always people tinkering on their boats, but by sunset the yard was mine. As long as I got up early in the morning, I wouldn't be caught. Besides, I preferred anything to suffocating under the pink duvets and greasy breakfasts of a B&B. At both entrances, the yard was protected by security lights that bathed the place in yellow as soon as anyone entered, but no one ever came. The only sounds were the slap of halyards against masts, the whistling wind and the occasional bird shriek. Boats possess as much character out of the water as in, and my neighbours – the blue motor cruiser, the deep-keeled ketch that looked so solid on her wooden scaffolding, the red trawler in for a serious repaint – made their presence felt in the dark. They were a strange fleet of unmanned craft sailing over the gravel. After eating dinner from a pot with my sailing knife, I'd fall asleep under the tent cover, barely conscious whether I was at sea or on land.

A sense of unreality ruled those days. So far, nothing had changed. I was preparing for sailing as I had so often in Keyhaven. But hanging over each moment was the aching, inescapable thought that my next voyage was not to be here to some river or creek, but across the mighty Channel to France. The Solent was behind me. The English Channel awaited. For a year I'd peered in through windows, looked through keyholes and cracks, maybe put my foot in the door, but now I was committed. I was going right in.

Was I scared? I'd always found the scariest part of anything the waiting, so maybe yes, a little. Then there were the Cassandras who always appear to heap on the fright. I knew them well from working as a journalist during the war in

Chechnya – people whose fear spread, whose indecision caused dangerous delays, who split groups and sapped the willingness to push on. These types liked to point out that you had so much to live for. They were full of advice about dangers they themselves hadn't experienced. Or they were people who honestly believed that the lines already drawn for us in the world really are the best and that to go beyond is automatically to invite disaster. On the whole I kept my plans quiet, but a few people heard enough to express dismay and ever so slightly condescending disapproval. One, dear old Jim at the boatyard, had said that only a 'bloody maniac' would undertake such a journey alone in a Wayfarer. Of course, I hadn't said it was I who was planning the trip, but his doom-filled speech about capsize, cold and exhaustion made an impression on several friends who most unfortunately happened to be there at the time. More recent and more serious were the admonitions of Ralph.

I came across Ralph because I'd been persuaded, against my will at first, that I ought to sail with a small outboard motor in reserve. This was for emergency use should I get becalmed while in the shipping lanes. Those lanes were ten miles wide and to drift without power in a boat so small was not something to countenance. A brief search for a motor to borrow took me to Ralph. He was a Wayfarer sailor of some renown and had a two-horsepower outboard available. Perfect. Except that Ralph, a stoical fellow who was cautious enough to wear a canoeing helmet while on sea voyages, instantly became suspicious.

In the first of a series of e-mail exchanges, Ralph asked if he might sail his boat along with mine. I declined, saying that would be impossible as I was determined to make the voyage unaccompanied not only by any other boat but also by any other person. No other way would do and even Adèle, who desperately wanted to come, knew she'd have to stay onshore. Ralph's reply was, 'The alarm bells are beginning to ring with regard to your proposed trip from Folkestone to Boulogne . . . Sailing a distance of over twenty-five miles through strong tides and busy shipping lanes single-handed in a Wayfarer and without any support is full of risk.' I was cut to the quick. At the final hurdle, someone had called my bluff. Lack of stability when sailing single-handed, getting lost, seasickness, strong winds – the dangers Ralph listed were legion. In his view, the only way to cross would be either with crew or with a safety boat in constant attendance, exactly, as I remembered, what Jim had said. 'How will you cope if fog comes down?' 'Have you a small suit of sails if the wind gets up?' 'How will you cope with any particularly drastic gear failure?' Every question Ralph put felt like an accusation.

My first sensation was one of utter failure and dismay. Ralph knew a lot about sailing and a lot about Wayfarers. Maybe he was right. But a bloody-minded resolve took over. Why should Ralph be right? He didn't know me; he didn't know my journey. I'd sailed in strong winds. I'd sailed more than thirty miles at a stretch. I'd sailed in wickedly rough water for a dinghy. Indeed, I'd sailed often when many yachts stayed at home and dinghies were nowhere to be seen. Provided that I picked my weather carefully, *Aquila* could take on the Channel. I said as much and Ralph's next e-mail was conciliatory. 'I am much reassured by the points you have made.' But he still wanted me to go with a support boat or to take on a crew. Ralph wrote that he would never 'contemplate crossing such a busy shipping lane solo and unaccompanied' and that 'by lending you my outboard, I would feel indirectly involved were anything disastrous to happen'. But the funny thing was that in calming Ralph's fears, I'd also calmed the last of my own. So it was that I replied, in all sincerity, that I respected his concerns and that if he didn't want to lend me the motor then he should not – I'd manage. The next e-mail said, 'I accept your assurances.' I could borrow not only the little Suzuki motor but also his GPS, a tiny computer that uses satellites to plot one's position, and a VHF radio, a walkie-talkie that would allow me, if needed, to contact the coastguard or anyone else on the sea. With these three items as back-up, I could deal with being becalmed, with getting lost in the fog and, God forbid, having to call for rescue. *Aquila* was ready.

During the long drive from Keyhaven to the Dover Straits with *Aquila* on her trailer behind, I entertained myself with the thought that in another era I might have been spared the need to cross by sea. During the next Ice Age the Channel could dry again and man, if he's still around, will tread where in ages past the valley ran and mammoths roamed.

Already a tug-of-war between land and sea is under way and every year the Channel changes shape, waves licking away at some parts of the coast, rocks tumbling down to force back the water at others. This is a struggle in which man, quite naturally, tries to back the side of land, as if dreaming, one day, of reversing the ancient invasion of the sea. Maybe all Channel crossings, in their different ways, are a matter of man shaking his fist at the sea, as if to say, 'Once we could walk across and we will again. Just stop us!' Certainly, the pioneers who first dreamed of building a permanent, solid link from

France to England saw their projects in this way. They were out to right a geographical wrong. Of course, the great hero of that particular battle was Thomé de Gamond. Until the Frenchman understood that the way to defeat the sea was by exploiting land's greatest strength (the continuous bed of chalk), the proposals for bridging the gap could only have made the god of the sea laugh. There'd been blueprints for an elegant but hopeless torchlit tunnel for horse and carriages; a ferry service of giant hot-air balloons; tubes suspended in mid-water from buoys; a submarine rail network running directly over the seabed; trains that rolled down a tube from one coast, then with the help of compressed air shot up the other, both trains and tube roofed with glass so that passengers could watch the fish or hulls of ships overhead . . . Even the sight of Thomé de Gamond diving for samples of the seabed would have made the sea god chuckle – at first.

What a quixotic figure this bourgeois and cerebral engineer must have struck as he went out to sea, already in his forties, accompanied only by his daughter and a few sailors from Boulogne. Diving remained a little understood activity in the 1850s and when Thomé de Gamond tried to use the latest watertight suit he almost suffocated. After that, despite making descents of thirty metres at a time, he trusted only his own home-made gadgets:

I prepared four sacks for the dive, each weighing 25 kilos, of which two were to be tied by ropes to the legs, at the ankles, and two others held by hand; in all, 100 kilos of extra weight. In addition, to make the return easier, I put together a string of 10 pig bladders, each divided in two little pockets, or air compartments, by a string around their middle . . . To protect my head, a cotton hat stuffed

209

with cloth was kept in place with a chin strap . . . I had to fill my ears with gauze mixed with butter and to cover the external part of the ears a large bandage, also buttered . . . I put a piece of buttered cotton in my nostrils, which though easily removed was enough to protect the nasal passages from the direct pressure of the water, which is unbearable at great depths. As for my mouth, I filled it at the very moment of diving, with a little spoon of olive oil, just as I'd seen fishermen do in the Mediterranean; a useful precaution, as it allows one to ease the pressure on the lungs as needed, making the exit of a few air bubbles easier, without having to open one's teeth and risking swallowing water. It was in this grotesque get-up that I threw myself into the deep.

The Channel Tunnel, finally built a long time after Thomé de Gamond died, was man's best shot in the land–sea war, but against that one tunnel the sea notched up any number of smaller victories every year. As, for example, in 1999, when hundreds of thousands of tons of the cliffs of Beachy Head avalanched 150 metres into the sea and man could only watch. That same year another huge fall took place almost opposite on the French coast between Le Havre and Dieppe, and French geologists said their coastline was retreating in places by fifty centimetres each year. Of course, man could and did fight back, but all his groynes and barricades were only as good as the will to maintain them, for this was certainly a contest of wills. And in such a contest the sea – this vast, corroding, destructive, moon-powered force – was difficult to beat.

One of the oddest battles took place daily at the promontory of Dungeness. It was while visiting the headland by the nuclear power station there that I'd noticed an earth mover filling trucks with shingle from the beach. Assuming that they were on some one-off job, I was surprised the next day to see the earth mover and trucks still at work. When one truck was full, another arrived. 'They take the shingle from here and carry it around the other side of Dungeness,' one of the fishermen by a tar-covered hut told me. I looked at him in surprise. 'That's right. They're moving the shingle up west. I watch them every day. Reckon they must get paid by the trip,' he added with a conspiratorial smile. 'I've seen down into the back of trucks from my bedroom window and I can tell you they're not always full – *not nearly.*'

What the trucks were doing, I learned, was just as the fisherman said. The prevailing south-west waves of the Channel pushed shingle relentlessly eastward, shifting the headland of Dungeness to the point where one day coastal towns such as Lydd, not to mention the power station, would be awash. In all, about 140,000 tons of the shingle travelled this way around the headland every year. In retaliation, lorries picked up about 60,000 tons of those stones and carried them back to where they'd started. The Sisyphean exercise just, but only just, kept the situation under control. Elsewhere on the coast, man had simply given up.

East of the Seven Sisters cliffs, I'd met a woman named Jean Faubert. Her hamlet of Birling Gap was falling into the sea. Some thirty years back, when she'd been young, the cliff was retreating about thirty centimetres a year. Now the sea worked quicker and the annual retreat was closer to a metre. Two of the eight cottages that once ran inland from the cliff had fallen over. A third was on the edge and had been vacated. Mrs Faubert's was two after that.

She and her neighbours were pleading with the authorities

for boulders to be placed at the bottom of the cliff to prevent further collapses, but neither the National Trust, which owned the property, the local council nor the national environmental powers wanted to take on the sea. 'The National Trust have fought tooth and nail against sea defences. They say it's a natural beach and that nothing must get in the way of that. We've formed a defence committee, but it's very hard to fight bureaucracy. One day, there'll be nothing left but the car park.'

Mrs Faubert had decorated her house with pretty jetsam – rope ends, shells, bottles, rocks – but she was in awe of the sea. 'The sea does have an effect on us. People just get drawn in here and then stand at the edge and stare. You look out and think how powerful it is. Just the fact that the tides go in and out and never stop. The shingle moves up and down by two or three metres sometimes. We're just helpless in the end.'

As a thousand years before, when King Canute, sitting on a beach near Southampton, made that famous, bitter joke against himself, the waves ruled. The time had come to go to sea.

In the end I fixed on departing from the long, straight beach at Hythe, one of those urban scraps along the coast from Folkestone. This way, when I set off, it would feel like any old trip on the Solent, but thirty miles or so of open sea later, I'd be arriving at one of Europe's major ports, Boulogne. My hosts were the people of the sea-front Hythe and Saltwood Sailing Club. These were not the usual dinghy clique, but the less ceremonial windsurfing crowd. Neither, to my satisfaction, were they overly nosy and I was left behind the clubhouse with *Aquila* to get on as I wished.

Saturday afternoon crowds swirled along the promenade: windsurfers, self-important in their wet suits; parents bored by complaining children; children bored by parents; precocious young girls; boys on bikes; old folk in hats and outsize sunglasses. The sailing club was preparing a barbecue. Cricket and tennis matches stuttered along in the park across the street. But all this swept past me, as insubstantial as if there'd been no one there at all. My sense of unreality was deepening all the time. Only one night and a few minutes of dragging *Aquila* down the shingle beach into the water separated me from my voyage, but I felt like a sleepwalker. I kept thinking (involuntarily): what am I doing? What is *Aquila-Gilliatt* doing? Why Hythe? Where am I going? A trickle of locals came along during the day to ask whether I really intended to cross the Channel, but my reply – that yes, that was right – echoed each time in my ears, as if someone else had been talking. From the promenade, I looked along the horizon. France was invisible, but my eyes were tuning in. Through binoculars, the haze yielded one ocean-going boat after another. Out there, about six miles away, was the first of the shipping lanes. I walked back to *Aquila*.

In addition to the mainsail, I had the genoa furled and the jib lashed down to the foredeck, both ready for use. As a precaution I'd borrowed a spare rudder and tiller from Tony Smee which I lashed down under one of the side benches. The radar reflector, a diamond-shaped metal object, was tied firmly to the top of the mast, instantly setting *Aquila* aside from other boats. To a non-sailor, my mast must have looked like a totem pole for warding off evil spirits, but to anyone who knew the sea, the reflector's presence was a badge of honour, a clear indication that I was headed for distant waters.

A further safeguard for the voyage was a strong inflatable sack shoved into the bow locker. The stern and bow compartments make the Wayfarer theoretically unsinkable, even when the rest of the boat is full of water, but in a collision or any other violent accident, the hatches might come off, or the boat might be holed. The inflated bag was meant to ensure that, whatever happened, at least part of *Aquila* would float, so, even wrecked, I'd have something to cling on to. Next, along with the usual gear of oars, bucket, anchor and tent, I tied the motor and a can of spare fuel securely to the floor at the stern, then began to stow the small items.

Chief among these was the navigation gear I'd need to make sure I crossed the shipping lanes correctly, then ended up at the right place on the French coast. The compass clipped into its place in the centre of the boat, the GPS and VHF, along with the plotting protractor, a screwdriver, foghorn, knife and a few bits of food, went into a storage bag right under where I'd sit. A box of offshore distress flares – red smoke for daytime rescue, red parachute flares for the night, white for warning against imminent collision – followed. Then, most important, I placed my chart in a plastic sleeve and slid it behind one of the side benches.

This chart was the last I'd had to buy, Admiralty chart 1892, showing the straits from Dover–Calais to Dungeness–Boulogne. Here, the world I was about to penetrate came alive in the usual meticulous detail: depth contours at just four metres off Hythe falling to around thirty mid-Channel, before diving to fifty, then rising sharply again to ten off the French coast; the eel-shaped, ship-wrecking banks mid-Channel of the Varne and the Ridge, or, as the French called the latter, Le Colbart; the crazy squiggles of underwater cables connecting the island to the Continent; the modest black dotted line representing the Channel Tunnel; the innumerable – worryingly innumerable – *Wks*, indicating wrecks. Then, on top, came my own annotations marking directions for the day.

My course was determined first by the international regulations requiring vessels to cross shipping lanes at a right angle. I also wanted to cross in the place where these lanes were narrowest – ten miles in all – which was between Folkestone and the headland of Cap Gris-Nez. The other main consideration was the tides, which, although not as strong as in the Solent, would be enough to push me off by several miles and so had to be factored into my calculations. My last markings were to circle the buoys I'd be likely to spot along the way. The Varne lightship and various buoys warned vessels away from the Varne and Ridge banks mid-Channel. The ZC2 yellow buoy, something of a landmark in Channel crossings, signalled the end of the shipping lanes on the French side. And, of course, there was the great lighthouse of Cap Gris-Nez, the first thing I'd see of France.

During the long day in Hythe, this chart, rolled and tucked into its place in the boat, was all there was to persuade me that I was not dreaming. There, in 2HB pencil, was my route. There, in the water just on the other side of the sailing clubhouse, was where it began.

My plan was to depart the next day, Sunday, at about 9 a.m. That was two hours after high water in Dover, which meant I'd catch the last of the eastward current to reach the shipping lanes. After, I could cross the lanes during the period of slack or weak currents, then finally head south-east down the ten-mile home stretch to Boulogne with a full-strength tide on my tail.

Everything now depended on the weather. The ideal conditions – Force 3 winds coming from the top half of the compass, good visibility and a smooth sea – were never going to happen. June had begun chaotically, a conga line of low-pressure systems from the Atlantic bringing bizarre combinations of sun, showers, strong winds, calms, winds whose direction was impossible to predict and equally erratic seas. There'd recently been the record low pressure for June recorded off Scotland and just a few days earlier a commemoration of the evacuation of Dunkirk was postponed due to gales (and, as it happened, those 'little ships' were a good deal bigger than mine).

However, the most recent weather maps had given me hope that Sunday would improve, with a shift in wind round to the west, which was ideal. Now I had only to check, praying that in these unstable conditions the forecast wouldn't have changed. From a red phone box on the sea front I dialled the recorded marine weather forecast. Two small girls with ice creams peered in. A pound coin jammed and I had to take out my knife. I tried to smile at the girls so they would not be alarmed. A voice came through. Good and bad news. According to the Met Office, Sunday's wind would indeed be westerly, but jacking up to Force 4, then 5. Waves would be moderate in size. On the scale used by the Met Office, moderate came before rough and very rough, but after calm, smooth and slight. All things being relative to boat size, moderate waves in a Force 5 meant a roller-coaster.

The forecast was right on the border between what I could and couldn't accept. As I scribbled the details into a notebook, I glanced out of the phone box. It was hard to believe that the baking sun and flat seas would be gone in twenty-four hours, but I knew from the Solent how like a chameleon the Channel was. I also knew I must go. Force 5 and moderate waves would be a hard ride, but something I'd often sailed, albeit on shorter journeys, before. From Monday, the weather was set really to deteriorate. Sunday, the day I'd been hoping and planning for, was my chance. I'd go.

It is extraordinary how simple life seems in the hours immediately before an event of which one really does not know the outcome. Earlier, I'd had *Aquila* to prepare, the sea to inspect, then the weather forecast to check. Now, in the dark, with the boat lying packed and primed, there was nothing left for me to do, nothing in the world, except sleep.

At the sailing club, the barbecue went on well into the night. Laughter, smoke and the sound of clinking glass wafted from the clubhouse to where *Aquila* lay and down on to the beach. The lights of a few ships twinkled far out in the Channel. Somewhere in the vastness, a new front travelled in and a low-pressure system edged towards Denmark, shifting the wind round to the west as it did. The tide was low. By the time I woke in the morning the water would be high, ready to sweep me to France.

I felt detached. When I climbed the stairs into the clubhouse to give thanks for the hospitality and to say goodbye, my mind remained elsewhere. The head of the club, Mark, treated me to one of those horror stories about an encounter off France with giant waves and an iron ore ship. A man named Wally did something similar, asking if I'd heard the term 'egg box' used to describe Channel waves. A woman, sentimental after a lot to drink, smiled at me with pity, as if she thought I'd not be coming back. The smoke choked me. I was glad to get back to *Aquila*, to bed down under shooting stars.

★

Early in the morning Wally helped me struggle with *Aquila* down the shingle into the sea. She proved almost too heavy. Once in the water, though, I could push her with one finger. I jumped aboard. Down rudder, down centreboard, in with the mainsail, unfurl the genoa. *Aquila* locked into the gentle breeze. Wally waved goodbye

I thought back to when I was a teenager in Spain and had to undergo an operation under general anaesthetic. I remembered trying to fight the sleep and resisting right up until I lost – well, almost, because in the very last moment I'd discovered a new pleasure in life: the pleasure of letting go. Count to ten, the anaesthetist said. I only made six. Pulling away from Hythe beach, this memory returned. Wally on the shingle, a cigarette on his lip. The sailing club, its flagpole bare. Apartment buildings full of retirees. The promenade empty except for early Sunday dog-walkers. The red phone box. There wasn't much, but just like the green gowns, bright lights, steel and tiling of that Spanish operating theatre, it was all I had and now I had to let go. In exchange for what? An empty horizon. Water rolling out of nowhere in oily swells. Nothing at all except the promise on the chart, untested so far, of another world.

I cruised in light winds along the coast. After an hour I'd passed Folkestone. Turning the headland, white cliffs appeared. I hadn't known they had them here too. They were ghostly and light. I was in position to find my crossing place for the shipping lanes. I must turn now or surely never cross at all. Bringing the tiller over was easy. *Aquila* wanted to go. I was with her. South-east, *Aquila-Gilliatt*. Whatever waits for us out there, we'll soon know. The wind rose. Folkestone began to disappear, the white cliffs floated, then they too began to disappear. I was really in the English Channel, the place between, the interruption, the nowhere land. Here, nothing could ever be permanent, or even stand still, not for a second. There was nothing to hold on to, and so, as on that day I surrendered to the anaesthetic, I understood, with pleasure, that the moment had come: I let go.

> Fast the white rocks faded from his view,
> And soon were lost in circumambient foam:
> And then, it may be, of his wish to roam
> Repented he.

So Byron wrote of Childe Harold at the start of his narrative. But then the spell of the Channel, that line separating old life from new, took its hold and the wanderer rejoiced:

> With thee, my bark, I'll swiftly go
> Athwart the foaming brine;
> Nor care what land thou bear'st me to
> So not again to mine.
> Welcome, welcome, ye dark-blue waves!

Amen, Childe Harold, I thought. Amen. As the seas piled up and the wind announced Force 5, as England sank, I felt the loneliness of exile and all the wild thrill of escape. I said the prayer, 'Lord, the sea is so wide and my boat is so small . . .' and didn't look back again.

Faced with an empty horizon you search for company. You find only yourself. You speak, but your words, having nowhere to go, sound unnaturally loud. You are alone. Apart from a fishing boat, where the men were tossing unwanted catch back into the sea, and an arriving ferry in Folkestone from Boulogne, I hadn't seen another person or boat since leaving Hythe. *Aquila-Gilliatt*, me, waves, current, wind. Nothing else. I'd expected a bazaar on the Channel: mad criss-crossing of ships; tourists hanging from the railings of ferries; fishing fleets in chase. Instead, solitude.

The wind rose steadily, bringing our speed from a couple of knots at the start to about five. In two and a half hours I was finally at the first shipping lane. Looking along the horizon to the east, up by Dover, I saw several vessels coming my way. Three appeared to be of medium size, but one I knew would be a monster. Even with the rest of the ship an indistinct square, her bow waves glinted white in the sun. With that day on the Dover–Calais ferry fresh in my mind, quite apart from all the times I'd looked out at the shipping from shore, I feared the worst.

The regulations put responsibility for avoiding collisions on vessels cutting across the shipping lanes, not those heading with the flow of traffic. However, having learned that a freighter moving at twenty-five knots would change from a dot on the horizon to a churning giant in only ten minutes, I was unsure, up to the day I sailed, how I would get out of the way. Even with the radar reflector at the top of the mast, I wondered whether *Aquila* would ever be seen, and in any case big ships, as far as I knew, did not, or could not, swerve. *Sailing: A Beginner's Guide* made grim reading: 'They probably can't see you, usually can't stop in time to keep from running you down, and might not know if they did.' A cartoon showed a yacht crossing the massive bows of a ship dubbed *Hexxon Intimidator*. The caption: 'But can HE see YOU?'

My first worry was the catamaran ferry between Folkestone and Boulogne. Fortunately, there was only one every few hours, unlike the relay between Dover and Calais. Still, this ferry, a spacecraft-shaped thing called a Seacat, moved at fifty knots or so and her wake alone would swallow *Aquila* whole. The one I'd seen arrive in Folkestone came out of the haze so fast that the whole thing appeared to be an optical illusion. Before the journey, I had taken the precaution of finding out the course taken by Seacats and plotting this on my chart with a thick dashed line. Provided I kept away from that, I could hope not to see another one the entire day.

The traffic in the shipping lanes, though, was unavoidable. Ten minutes had elapsed since I'd spotted that group near Dover and now they were all close. The monster turned out to be a container ship, her hull black, bridge white and containers, stacked like play bricks, in red, yellow and blue.

At this point, I'd once imagined being forced into hair's-breadth escapes, ships rearing up, blocking the sun and knocking the wind from my sails. However, I could see as soon as the ships were close that at their speed – at least four times faster than my own – I had absolutely no chance of a collision at all. All I had to do was slow down a little more, by spilling the wind from the sails, or turning slightly up into the wind, and I was guaranteed to see the oncoming vessels pass well in front. All the time, I checked the horizon for others. There were none visible, which meant I could continue. When the next group did arrive -- and there was almost certainly another group just over the horizon – the chances were that I'd have made sufficient forward progress for these new ships to pass behind. This was less like crossing a motor-way, as was so often said, and more like crossing a desert railway. Empty silence, then a flurry of hurtling wagons, then empty silence.

Crossing grew more complicated, as I discovered later, when two sets of shipping approached at the same time. That made the decision whether to continue harder, for you risked missing one ship, only to run into the path of the next, or the one after that. However, I found that even in these cases there would always be long gaps somewhere. Ships do not bunch up. If I wanted to let all the danger pass, I could simply turn around and go back the way I had come for a while, then return to my original position, all the ships I'd seen before now having gone. In a less extreme strategy I could continue moving forward and only when a collision course appeared likely turn *Aquila* down the shipping lane in the same direction as the oncoming vessel. That gave the ship's helmsman a clear indication I was not going to try to cut across his bows and that for him it was safe to keep going straight. Within minutes the ship would have passed and I could turn again and resume my original course.

Constantly I searched the horizon. From my eye level, between one and 1.5 metres above the sea, the horizon appeared only two and a half miles away, although large ships poked up a good ten miles off, depending on visibility. Already when a ship was at medium range, say five miles (about fifteen minutes away), it was time to start judging whether she and *Aquila* could collide. The easiest way was just to watch the angle of the oncoming bows. If the bows were more or less in symmetry, then the ship was aiming at me. If the starboard bow was more visible than the port, then the ship would hopefully pass in front, and if more of the port bow was clear, she would pass behind. The actual mayhem of a collision must be over quickly, but the build-up could not be slower. In fact, it is in many ways the same dangerous size and speed of the ships that make them safe. Unlike yachts and powerboats during a busy day on the Solent, these big ships travel in predictable lines. Their bulk, which would crush a yacht like a matchbox underfoot, makes them visible from far away. Their relentless speed means that they disappear as quickly as they arrive.

The impersonal, brutal threat of the freighters and tankers meant for me that they barely counted as ships – they might as well have been reefs or icebergs. Surely there were people aboard, but I'd never see them. And although our vessels were on the same part of the chart, we inhabited different, parallel worlds. Yes, right in the middle of the world's busiest shipping lane, it was very easy to feel alone.

Aquila ran south-east, 130 degrees as always, riding a sea as rhythmical as a merry-go-round. I knew what Wally had meant about the egg box. In the Solent with a strong wind against that four-knot current you got an egg box – densely packed steep little waves that punched *Aquila* so hard she staggered. In the open Channel, though, something else was going on. Here, the waves came in a pattern: big, hump-backed, black-blue sea, rolling out of the west in rows, about seven at a time. This was a swell born in the Atlantic. It poured into the Channel with the westerly winds and would go on eastwards, unchecked, until smashing against France – some breakwater, the rocky foot of a cliff, the gentle gradient of a beach or a holiday-maker's legs.

The worst place to take a wave is on the side of a boat, but that was the way the swell was coming and, for the first couple of hours, *Aquila* managed fine. Each wave appeared darkly over my shoulders, disappeared a second later under *Aquila*'s polished hull, then slipped out on the other side, rushing noiselessly on towards self-destruction.

As the wind grew and the tide stretched to a westward flow, contrary to the wind, the sea began to have fun. By the time we were halfway (I knew where we were because I could see the Colbart North buoy a couple of miles up to my west) the swell was no longer so round. The sides were steeper and bigger. When waves passed underneath, *Aquila* rose high in the air and sometimes, as the swell rushed away on the other side, my view of that horizon was blocked. The sea surface that had begun as silk looked more like a ragged old coat.

As the wind went up, my sails came down. From full main and genoa at the start, I'd moved to one reef in the main, then to jib instead of genoa, then, as white horses and spray began to fleck the sea, to all three reefs in the main. Even so, we were touching the excellent speed of six knots. 'A lot easier than the Solent egg boxes, eh?' I asked *Aquila*. Quite suddenly – at sea things nearly always go wrong quite suddenly – one wave, a bank of water just like every other, rose up to our windward side, just like every other, and then, unlike all the others, did not slip underneath. In a single, frightening moment, this was what I saw: a mass of smooth green water thump against *Aquila*; a bathtub's worth of sea cascade over me and the gunwale into the boat; *Aquila* jerk violently to leeward as the weight of the wave, combined with the wind, pushed her over. That's it, I thought: capsize. We're going to flip. Another swell was rolling in at us, only seconds from impact, but I had time to throw my weight backwards, let the mainsail free and turn the rudder sharply into the wind and swell. Somehow the words of old Jim, practically the first thing he'd ever told me, played in my head: 'Remember if you're ever in real trouble, let that mainsail fly.' I'd done just that – opened my clenched hand and let the mainsheet snake out, removing in two seconds all the wind from the sail – and we were saved.

I still had to be quick. As long as we were pointed up, we wouldn't easily be overwhelmed, but as long as all the water remained in the boat we were heavy, hard to manoeuvre, and so at risk. The first concern was to get the worst of the water out. I hove to, then pumped for about a minute, sending the sea that had come in so green shooting from the discharge pipe in frothy silver spurts. Next, I had to further reduce sail. I could no longer balance *Aquila* safely as she was. Scrambling up by the mast, I dropped the jib and tied it down. I was using just the deep-reefed main now. Then, opening up the self-bailers (the two valves cut into the bottom of the boat), I took in the mainsail and sailed off on a broad reach. That gave us top speed, making the self-bailers work better, and put the oncoming waves more to our stern. The self-bailers sucked, the water swilling around the floorboards vanished back into the Channel and in a few minutes *Aquila* was empty.

Nothing was quite the same after. The compass invited us back on course. The horizon asked us to come deeper. The waves kept rolling in. Halfway. France was no more than a grey line, England was gone. But it didn't feel like halfway. The seas were rising, I still had five miles of the second shipping lane to cross and after that the ten miles from Cap Gris-Nez to Boulogne, the first shelter on all that coast.

Many of the waves still slid under *Aquila*, but about one in seven were the kind that might break and could only be met head-on. With one eye always to starboard, I steered to the dance of the sea, a straight run south-east with a hundred little side-steps up and down the waves. Usually I was able to turn into the bigger waves in time to rise over, then down the other side. Sometimes the oncoming side was so steep that *Aquila* hung on the top, half out of the water like a statue, then thudded down the back side to meet the next. Occasionally she was unable to rise in time and the top of the wave broke on her bows and rushed over the foredeck. At other times, a following wave came so close after the first one that she ploughed nose-first into the water. Down she'd go. Hull shuddering, woodwork shining under the flood of sea. Then the bow would burst back, water cascading. I'd forgotten how much noise there is when sailing gets rough. There was nothing peaceful about the mainsail cracking when I luffed, or the creak of rigging in the gusts, or the relentless singing of the wind, or, above all, the crash of water against the bow. Even the sea, previously silent, had begun to groan.

As the lines between boat, sailor and sea blurred, I no longer saw myself as a separate entity but rather as a collection of implements, the latest set of equipment for *Aquila*. My arms were robot limbs, unquestioning, in constant and minute readjustment of the tiller and mainsheet control; my trunk was devoted only to balancing the boat; my eyes searched for incoming waves, gusts and ships; my feet and legs, holding on to special straps, anchored the machinery and boat; my mind – I thought of nothing except the sails, the balance and the sea just upwind. Likewise our separation from the water. On a yacht, the sailor can almost always duck inside and close the hatches. At the other extreme, the liner passenger can sit in a cinema or go shopping, even in the greatest storm. On *Aquila*, though, there was not a dry surface and nor would there be. Every inch, inside and outside, shone wet. The self-bailers never stopped working. My hair was soaked, my oilskins dripping. And every few minutes, in came more water. The greatest noise in all that whistling and roaring was the water punching my face. I thought of all the *Wk*s on the chart. I'd already passed over many of them and in that final stretch south along the French coast I'd be sailing over what amounted to a graveyard. It wasn't so hard to imagine how they happened.

What a strange companion the sea is – more awesome than intimate, more god-like than friendly. In dreamy moments, I took my eyes off my immediate surroundings and snatched glimpses of the wider scene. Maybe a person walking alone through uninhabited places – a moor, mountains, a desert – could share what I felt then. I was in a savage landscape, but this was a desert that heaved and jumped every second, a mountain that rolled, a moor that tumbled.

When a seagull appeared from this wilderness, I was happy. Head cocked, wings set like sails, he skimmed the waves, made a few passes by *Aquila* and shot away. The first living thing I'd seen for four hours. 'A friend, *Aquila*,' I said, and I knew then we'd make it.

A red flag. The sight, when I'd been half mesmerized by the monotony of water, water and still more water, filled me with wonder. A tattered, faded red flag waving from the surface right ahead of *Aquila*. I was so unprepared that only fantastic explanations came to mind: the flag was the top of a sunken ship, or represented a claim somebody was making on that scrap of sea . . . By the time my mind returned to reality and I realized of course that the flag was attached to a small buoy left by a fisherman to mark his pots, *Aquila* and I had left the curious and brave little pennant behind.

But now I was awake. Fishing was banned in the traffic zone, so that could only mean that I'd left the second shipping lane. Indeed, about three miles ahead to the east was the lighthouse of Cap Gris-Nez. France! Being daylight, there was no sign of the light, but the tower, the only structure visible along the entire coastline from that distance, rose from the cliffs clear as a line on a blank page. At once I thought of the Lizard lighthouse, old keeper Eddie Mathews and the day I'd decided to explore this sea. I remembered his telling me that sailors of small craft were the most sorry to see lighthouse keepers go, because 'it's especially them that like to know somebody is up there watching – a pair of human eyes'. Now, on my first occasion to see a lighthouse properly from the sea, I didn't care. Maybe, against all the odds, some old French keeper was looking down, but did it matter? The lighthouse, by telling me where I was, had already done its job, and for that alone I was full of thanks.

The buoy known as ZC2 was slightly to my north-east – I'd been off course by half a mile or so – so the time had come to change direction to a bearing of 153 degrees and head along the coast for Boulogne. The change put me closer to the wind and also more into the waves. The ride was getting bumpier all the time. But I had the full ebb tide coming right from behind now, adding a good two knots of speed, so if all went well I'd reach Boulogne in less than two hours. France. France. France. I had to keep repeating this. Adèle would be waiting on the breakwater in Boulogne – at least I hoped so. I wondered how far out she'd be able to spot my sail. Not far, probably. Even at two miles, *Aquila* was a speck.

The flags! The fact that I was now in French waters reminded me that by now I should have been flying two flags, one a Red Ensign, because my boat was registered in Britain, and also, as a sign of courtesy as soon as I entered French waters, a small Tricolour. I'd had the flags neatly folded, ready for use, in a bag under one of the benches, but had been too preoccupied to remember. The etiquette required me to attach the ensign to my starboard shroud and the Tricolour to the port shroud, the position of secondary honour. Had I had any other flags, they too would have found their place in positions of third and fourth honour and so on. But even now that I'd remembered my duties, I didn't care to carry them out. To raise the flags would mean heaving-to, then clambering around by the shrouds, and in this sea, where the swell had become ever more irregular and broken, that didn't entice. So, I thought, to hell with the flags.

I'd never wanted them anyway. The Red Ensign was allowed because *Aquila* was on the books of the Small Ships Registry, but I wasn't British and just the idea of the ensign made me uncomfortable. At first, I'd been intending not to bring one at all. After all, the sea, I'd always imagined, was the one place where flags really didn't matter. There might be lines drawn on charts, but the borders were invisible. There were no checkpoints and never could be. Tides, waves and fish came and went as they pleased. So why not boats and sailors too? By crossing the Channel, it seemed to me, I would have the right to claim my place as a citizen of the sea.

One phone call to the RYA and consultation of a few

manuals had shot away my Utopia. Flags, I was told, were required. Not only that, but as an American citizen I should on arriving in Boulogne raise a third flag, this time yellow, to indicate to the Customs authorities that their inspection was required. The quarantine flag, it was called. Then, for foreign boats in French ports, there were all manner of legal pitfalls of which I had to be aware. Unlike Britain, where there was no law on the matter at all, the French followed EU regulations on how far small boats could go from a coast. *Aquila* was somewhere in a poorly defined area between boats for the sea and boats for protected waters, so there might be difficulties with zealous officials. Beyond that, there were Byzantine questions about whether VAT had been paid on the purchase of the visiting vessel, and exacting demands about what kind of safety equipment had to be carried, again depending on where the boat would go. My sea had begun looking rather less free.

In the days when Britannia really did rule the waves, England had enforced the extraordinary edict that all shipping, English and foreign, must salute royal ships. The command, which required dipping one's flag in submission, exempted no one in the 'Narrow Seas', not even foreign royalty and not even by the French coast. Some captains thumbed their noses – a fifteenth-century English privateer recorded having ordered a foreign fleet to strike its colours 'in the name of the King of England, and they bade me shit in the name of the King of England' – but the Royal Navy was authorized to sink ships that disobeyed. In the seventeenth century, even poor old Christian IV, the King of Denmark, was humiliated into having to lower his flags while visiting England with his fleet. The sole echo today of those brazen flag patrols is that a British boat should dip its ensign to a Royal Navy vessel and expect the warship to dip its White Ensign in response. Well, that and an awful lot of paperwork.

By the time I left, my little package of documents in sealed plastic wrapping included passport, insurance papers for the boat, proof of purchase and price (I'd finally ascertained that proof of having paid V A T probably wasn't needed for a boat costing so little), V H F radio operator's certificate, the boat's official registration card and, just in case, a certificate for my navigation course. To that I had reluctantly added the pair of little flags.

Yet I'd still forgotten to declare my allegiance on crossing the hidden line. Well, I was glad. *Aquila* didn't need flags, the sea didn't want them and I wouldn't have them. To hell with the flags. I *was* a citizen of the Channel now.

Audresselles, Ambleteuse, Wimereux. Rolling and punching through waves, I passed them all, those sleepy, dignified little resorts in the dunes and fields stretching between Cap Gris-Nez and Boulogne. I thought of the people there, maybe finishing late Sunday lunches, maybe napping in the great big sea-front hotel of Wimereux, maybe making use of the low tide to walk for miles over cool, packed sand. All I could see, though, were the rough shapes of the towns, and I doubted whether anyone onshore could see me. On the chart I passed half a dozen wrecks, an explosives dump and some old under-water cables, but I saw none of that either. Only the Channel chop, the splash from the bow and my goal, slowly coming into focus, the outer breakwater of Boulogne.

A yacht sailed past in the other direction, but closer inland, reaching against the current. A small freighter passed ahead, making for Boulogne. I could see clearly the walls of the outer harbour. As I hit shallower water, the waves suddenly got choppier, a true mess, and I no longer sailed in anything close to a straight line. Weaving, dipping and climbing, this was a hard finish. But it was the finish. I could see people fishing with great long rods from the harbour walls. Suddenly, flat water. I was inside Boulogne. I'd been at sea seven hours.

The outer harbour of Boulogne, called the Rade Carnot, covers almost four square miles. I sailed right across, making for the next set of walls, beyond which hid the inner Bassin de Marée. Two towers, one red, one green, stood on the breakwaters marking the entrance. Under the red tower, there were many people who had come for the air and to watch the sea. A small figure among the crowd began to jump and wave. Adèle. She was there. Leaning over the gunwale, I waved in return.

Still some sailing to do though. Respect the sea to the end, for nothing is easier than to run into difficulties just when the voyage feels over. Even the neaps tide falls almost 4.5 metres in Boulogne and because we were at low water the walls of the breakwater towered over *Aquila* as I entered the inner harbour. Adèle was running along the wall, keeping pace. Many heads poked over. Puzzled heads. What was this tiny boat doing? The day had become rather pleasant. The sun was out. But I was dressed in boots and oilskins. A rope was tied around my waist. The mainsail was reefed. The whole boat glistened with sea water. Where had I been?

The wind, having seen me safely in, said goodbye. Inside these walls all was calm. Quick. Untie that engine. It had lain so patiently on the floor all the way. In two minutes I had the little outboard free, attached to the transom of *Aquila* and running. Just in time, for the Bassin de Marée was a busy place, home to Boulogne's yachts, fishing boats and the Seacat. No good drifting around in there. The motor made a friendly gurgle. The fishing fleet was over on the left, underneath stalls selling their catch from that day. Yachts were on the right. There was the pontoon. I dropped the mainsail, cut the motor and floated in without a noise. Adèle came running. She had champagne.

Berthed between big yachts, *Aquila* was at once the object of curiosity. 'A radar reflector? Why carry that just for camping along the coast?' asked a man just off his fifty-footer. I answered in an offhand way that no, I wouldn't have the reflector for camping, only for the shipping lanes. He nodded silently. A Dutch yachtsman on holiday from his job as a big ship captain informed me that radar reflectors might in any case be of no use because crews often didn't bother to look at their radar screen. The harbourmaster, too polite to say more, noted only, '*Il est petit, votre bâteau.*' Suddenly unable to contain my laughter, I replied, '*Petit, mais . . .*' I couldn't find the word and instead raised a fist. '*Efficace,*' the harbourmaster suggested, laughing back. '*Oui, très efficace,*' I replied. Not the word I wanted, but it would do. The word I wanted probably didn't exist, not in any language, and even if it did, *Aquila-Gilliatt* deserved something new.

Saying goodbye to our new friends, Adèle and I booked into a cheap hotel by the harbour for the night. The champagne went quickly.

6

B y morning, the weather was foul. Leaving the port at my back, I climbed up to the cathedral in the old quarter. The sky was as cold and grey as the cobbles underfoot and fog ate at the cathedral's dome. I had an appointment to keep and once inside I made straight for a corner at the back. I found her at once: Our Lady of the Great Return.

The life-size statue of Mary sat – a gold heart in her left hand, the Christ child, who held a gold-banded orb, in her right – in a wooden boat about the size of a tub. Both figures and the boat, which had a bow like a fishing smack, were painted white, and had been placed on top of a small wagon with rubber tyres.

The cult of this seafaring Mary had begun with the miraculous arrival in Boulogne in the year 636 of a boat with no sails and no crew, save a wooden statue of the Virgin. Now, in addition to the statue on the wagon, the cathedral housed a smaller version in Lebanese cedar in one of the side chapels, and a more Baroque creation, including two angels on board, sailing through a tempest carved over one of the altars. What was supposedly a surviving fragment of the original statue's hand took pride of place in the cathedral crypt. The relic, a tiny piece of wood, had been inserted into the top of a full-size polished brass hand resting gruesomely on a red velvet cushion.

I preferred the white figures. Apart from ending so abruptly at the stern, their boat had a businesslike mien. Like *Aquila*, the bow was high and strong. Also like *Aquila*, the hull was made in a similar design of overlapping planks. This statue, along with three similar ones, had been dragged all over France in a pilgrimage-cum-road show that lasted from 1943 to 1948. Huge crowds – 100,000 people at one stop in 1946 – used to gather. Since then, the boat had often been wheeled out for processions in the streets and along the quay of Boulogne. Today the cathedral was all but empty. There was no one to see Notre-Dame-du-Grand-Retour except a cleaner, noisily scraping wax from a candle tray, and me.

It was to this Mary I had come to give thanks for my voyage. Mary of the Channel, Mary of Small Boats. I knelt and prayed. Then, as soon as the cleaner left, I took a long white candle and placed it alone, like a lighthouse, in the middle of the empty tray.

That afternoon I took a bus from Boulogne, got out at a village inland and walked a couple of miles through rolling fields of wheat to Cap Gris-Nez. Old German bunkers loomed from the poppies. One had been turned into a cowshed. But everything else reminded me of my walk a year and a half before to the Lizard light. That had been in winter, but on this unseasonal June day the wind blew as hard, drizzle wormed into my skin and, as I approached the Cap Gris-Nez tower from a distance, I half expected Eddie Mathews, mug of tea in hand, to greet me at the door. The circle that had begun in Cornwall was closing.

Cap Gris-Nez was inhabited, though not by a lighthouse keeper. While the French, unlike the British, were retaining a handful of keepers in remote areas, just to preserve the profession, this tower had been automated long before. Now,

Cap Gris-Nez was important as a coastguard station and true life resided not in the tower's light but in the restless, sweeping arms of a radar. Clumps of antennae bristled in the most unlikely shapes from a compound beneath the lighthouse. Inside, there would be coastguards watching the Dover Straits on screens, but I could see no sign of human life and an iron gate barred my way. The compound, like the cowshed, had once been a German bunker.

Excitement and nerves took over. For two winters and two summers I'd searched for the heart of the Channel and the key, I was sure, lay right here. Once, as at the Lizard lighthouse, I'd have taken Cap Gris-Nez, with its science fiction atmosphere, as proof that this storied body of water was losing its soul. Certainly things had looked that way. The old sinews of the Channel – the shipyards, liners, navies, tourist resorts and fishing fleets – were diminished, or already gone, and today the symbol of this sea was, of all things, a train. So I could easily have arrived at Cap Gris-Nez and seen only a reflection of the Lizard, a grim symmetry on two sides of a soulless sea.

Instead, I felt nothing but elation, for this place had finally proved right the hunch I'd had all along: that the secrets of the Channel could be found only at sea, not on land. Up here, I saw an empty tower and an orchard of humming antennae, but out there with *Aquila* the day before there'd been another Cap Gris-Nez – a thrilling first landmark of France, a warning of danger, but also the promise of safety. That had been the Channel I'd hoped so much to discover and I'd found it at last.

Maybe in the past anyone could get a taste of the sea, even while on land. The fabric of the coasts was so rich then. Now it was different. The sea didn't come to you – you had to go to the sea. But that was all. The heart of the Channel hadn't died. It was right out there, three miles off Cap Gris-Nez in the waves. Anyone with a boat – never mind the size – could check.

As I walked back through the poppies and wheat, one last riddle gnawed. With my pilgrimage to the lighthouse over, I wondered what to do next. I'd never given much thought to anything beyond arriving with *Aquila* in France and now here I was. The sensible thing, I supposed, would be to hop on the Seacat to Folkestone, fetch the car from Hythe, come back and tow *Aquila* home. After all, there was no need for more risks once the journey was done. But then – and it was this that gnawed – was my journey really done?

Had I crossed a lake – Lake Superior, say, which is as big as the Channel – I might have hung up my oilskins and said enough is enough. But on the sea, things are different. Because every ocean and sea connects, even the humblest part – even that part between Hythe and Boulogne – is a door to the furthest reaches of the world. That is why the sea seems endless, why the sea makes men dream. My aim had been only to cross the Channel, but, like the oceans and seas, each dream leads to another, and now that I'd completed one small journey, a second much greater had to begin. From the Channel, launching place of so many voyages, this was a parting gift.

There'd be no ferry. I would go back to Boulogne to get *Aquila-Gilliatt* ready and we'd return to England under sail. This time, with Adèle. And then? Wherever water flowed. I had been marooned, but now I was free.

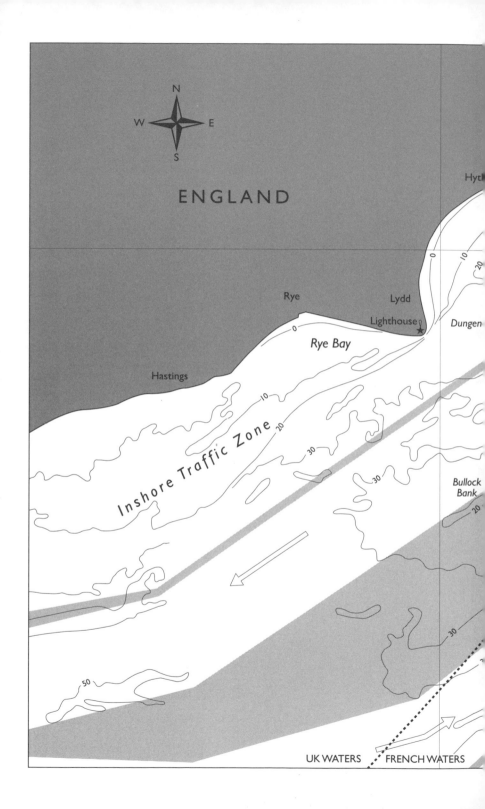